85 DRAWINGS

ABOUT THE **HERE** AND **HEREAFTER**

by **Phil Saint**

AUTHOR-ARTIST

DOVE Christian Books
Melbourne, Florida

Published by
DOVE Christian Books
P.O. Box 36-0122, Melbourne, FL 32936
Melbourne, Florida

DEDICATION

Many wonderful people have made a very positive contribution to this book. Pastors and others have studied them, and have made valuable suggestions. My great hero of bygone days was Herbert Johnson, a consummate master of expression, action, dramatic situations, and humor. My dear old dad and my precious mother had an influence on my life for which I shall be eternally grateful. Cartooning is very different from making stained glass windows; but both Dad and I have always endeavored to honor and glorify Jesus our Lord in our art.

Gaylord DuBois, professional writer and spirit-filled Christian, and Mary, his talented wife, have made a significant contribution to many pages of copy and to the overall tone of the message.

I am grateful to God and to them for their valuable editorial assistance.

The one who has made the greatest contribution to this book is Ruth, my sweet, happy, long-suffering wife. She is among the few who know how to suffer long — and be kind, as the Bible puts it. Her patience and grace have been wonderful to see, as I have gotten up in the middle of the night to draw, or have disrupted the family schedule to respond to a sudden inspiration. Ruth's suggestions about the text have been super. I have changed and rewritten a number of paragraphs based on her wise insights, given to her by the Holy Spirit.

So I would like to dedicate this book to her, a heart-warming companion, a scrumptious cook, and a veteran missionary in her own right. If she ever writes a book on "missionaries I have known," meaning me, you will see what I mean!

FOREWORD

If one picture is worth a thousand words, I would have to rewrite the encyclopedia to match what Phil Saint has done with his cartoons.

I first met Phil in the early 50's. At the insistence of my parents I spent a few weeks one summer at Word of Life Camp in New York State. Phil was on staff that summer and regarded by all as something of a Kingdom hero. His brother, Nate, was heading to Equador to minister to the savage Auca Indians. His sister, Rachel, was an equally famous Bible translator with Wycliffe Bible Translators. To mention the Saint family in evangelical circles was to get an automatic "Aaahhh!" response.

I still feel that way when I think of the Saints.

Nate was martyred by the Aucas in the mid-fifties. Rachel followed him into the jungle and was instrumental in seeing many of the tribe, including the ones who actually murdered her brother, accept Jesus Christ as Lord. Phil, a missionary in Argentina, actually baptized his brother's murderers in the same river where they found Nate's body. It's a spine-tingling story. Much of it is told in Phil's excellent book, *Amazing Saints* (Logos).

But there is more to Phil's life than being a missionary, artist and preacher. He has a prophet's streak as well. And when he had a personal encounter with the Holy Spirit several years ago, his prophetic gift began to emerge in his cartoons.

I have urged him, on several occasions, to stop doodling and get his work published. This is his first effort. Some of the cartoons will entertain. Others will evoke a solemn nod from the reader. All will prod into the heart of any individual involved in Kingdom activities.

You'll also meet Phil in these cartoons. He's part fundamentalist, part charismatic, part iconoclast, part shepherd. Most of all, he's a dear friend who has been touched by the Holy Spirit — whose very life is dedicated to serving the Lord Jesus Christ.

Read a while. Chuckle. Get a little bit angry. But do not miss the truth. It's there — in each one of these funny little cartoons.

Jamie Buckingham
Melbourne, Florida

TABLE OF CONTENTS

Deep in the heart of every one of us there is a child — a child who needs comfort and a parent's all-embracing protection. The world has lost its Parent. Terror of surrounding darkness grips its mind. Somewhere, our poor little world has lost even its security blanket.

Past generations *did* have a false security; viz., atheistic faith that humanity could eventually find its way out of every dark, threatening woods. Yesterday looked to "science" for every solution — and only this morning have we awakened to the horror of a nuclear arms race. The ugly menacing forest of proliferating weapons continues to grow at an alarming pace!

The fear, the distress, is because all hopeful formulas fail in the face of mankind's basic selfishness and depravity. Only He who is *the Way*, Jesus Christ, can lead humanity out of the coming destruction.

Two years after the war with Japan, I stood surveying the devastation that was once Hiroshima — an entire city instantly destroyed by one A-bomb. Only the massive walls of two buildings stood like grave stones in the midst of what had once been a beautiful city. But atomic weapons have grown apace; and today the forest of cataclysmic missiles has achieved staggering proportions.

It is high time for men and women to follow the path, Christ Jesus, turning their backs on the sinister moon of atomic war that hangs menacingly in the end-time sky.

Jesus said, "I am the Way, the Truth, and the Life. No one comes to the Father except through me."[1] He also said, "Come to me, all you who are weary and burdened, and I will give you rest. Take my yoke upon you and learn of me, for I am gentle and humble in heart, and you will find rest for your souls. For my yoke is easy and my burden is light."[2] We need not continue in our lost condition. Each one of us, individually, can live, even in this apocalyptical world, with a settled peace in our hearts, through Him who is the Prince of Peace.

[1]John 14:6   [2]Matthew 11:28

BABE IN THE WOODS

A LOOK AT THE FUTURE

10

DANGER AT THE WATER HOLE

11

The USS FREE ENTERPRISE is a grand old ship with a proud history. The founders of our nation designed its famous blueprint — the constitution. They built it to carry a mighty population to a place of peace and prosperity — and in times past, it has proved the most successful political system ever devised by men. Today it is bound for *pre-planned shipwreck.*

Who planned it? Who profits from it? No one but certain powerful, little seen, plotters who more and more control international finances and commerce, and who increasingly dominate the communications media and the political trends of our nation and others as well. Through mounting government debt, and through an army of well-paid lobbyists, they bring about political action — or inaction — to suit their secret plans for world power.

They effectively wage a quiet, hidden war on free enterprise. Their big guns are aimed at true democracy, patriotism, social morality, and the Christian faith, which is the basis of all that is good. Through their manipulation of the press, the moving picture industry, and television, the public has been subtly conditioned to despise the so-called "victorian virtues."

Personal honesty, personal thrift, and personal savings founded American free enterprise; but now, more and more, we are being encouraged to live beyond our means. Few are alarmed by soaring private and public debt — just alarmed at the galloping inflation that is eating up wages and buying power — that is the result! In this country, individuals owe over a trillion dollars, according to some experts. The national debt is now beyond comprehension.

Unless the course of our present financial system is changed, and drastic measures of economy are resorted to, disaster is certain. The one-worlders are now openly talking of an international system of finance, where no one will be able to buy or sell without the mark of the beast prophesied in the Holy Bible centuries ago.[1] Praise God, we bear the mark of Jesus Christ, who will come again to rule in righteousness and love! Then, debts, inflation, and poverty will be known no more![2]

[1]Revelation 13:16   [2]Micah 4:4

PRE-PLANNED SHIPWRECK

13

There is a tropical tree that sends down limbs that on reaching the ground form roots and in fact, become another tree, while still connected to the parent trunk. In this cartoon, it serves as an illustration of how Satan extends his control over human institutions such as the home, the school, the church, and government.

This ideological tree is a fact, not a dream. It is a political octopus that won't go away. It keeps spreading over God's green earth.

As true followers of Jesus Christ, we must fight this monster with all the strength that God gives. Our responsibility is not limited to our own personal lives; we have the additional duty of being the "salt of the *earth*" and the *"light* of the *world,"* fighting evil in our social and political environment.

The means we use must be dictated by the Holy Spirit and empowered by prayer. Our greatest weapon against the enemy is the sword of the Spirit, the Word of God (here pictured as a spiritual power saw).* This invincible weapon will cut through the devil's paralyzing grip. The home, the individual and the society that will heed God's truth can be free!

The impact of the church of Christ on society can and must be felt. It played a major part in the building of this great nation, and shook the Roman Empire to its very foundations back in the days after Pentecost. It is the only force that can preserve liberty in these days when every man-made institution is feeling the stifling grip of this unseen, but very real monster.

Some of us have, in other days, said, "I just preach the gospel; I don't get into politics." This may sound very pious, but it is not in accord with what we find in the Bible. Abraham got into "politics" when he formed his servants into an army and rescued Lot and the people of Sodom from enemies that had defeated them in battle and carried them away captive. Daniel spent his whole life in politics, serving as prime minister of Babylon and continuing as a force for righteousness in the same capacity under the Medes and Persians. Esther became the queen of a king over a great empire and by heroic action saved the Jews as a nation, with her uncle Mordecai becoming a powerful figure in government. Joseph was for many years supreme ruler of Egypt, placed there by a divine act of God.

If there ever was a time in the history of the world when we needed men of God in high places and an army of Christians who are against evil in government, it is now!

*Ephesians 6:17

14

CUTTING THE BANYAN TREE

We sometimes talk about the "patience of Job." I think there is another good candidate for first prize when it comes to patience — the American taxpayer. It is incredible how United States citizens have meekly pedalled the government bicycle, wearing themselves out paying taxes and more taxes, to sustain a spend-thrift political give-away program. It would seem at last, that the situation might change, may it be so!

Little by little, over the past years, the social planners have been slipping over on us a welfare state that dreams of running, not only the government, without our consent, but of running our private lives as well. All this is being done with great sums of money — ours!

With every year that has passed, more and more free-loaders and political parasites have climbed on the bandwagon of government handouts. The fat lady is distributing more and more money to people who present themselves as needing medical help, educational subsidies, unemployment assistance, and just plain everyday support for living. There are "abandoned" mothers whose husbands have disappeared, yet they have another baby every year. There are "students" who do not study, who have been caught receiving *two* student grants at the same time, and an army of people who for one reason or another receive continual support from the government, although they seem to be quite able to work.

Now nobody is suggesting that we cut off help for those who are really unable to care for themselves; but the day has come when we must stop handing out money to people who *can* work, but *won't*. The Bible says, "If a man will not work, neither shall he eat."* It is time to crack down on unprincipled politicians who use hardworking taxpayers' money to buy votes for themselves, and thus perpetuate a socialistic system that is weakening our country, and pushing us into national bankruptcy. The government should be the first entity to set an example of honesty, efficiency, and solvency.

*2 Thessalonians 3:10

BICYCLE BUILT FOR TWO

The old homestead, called the United States of America, once cared for with so much patriotism and pride, has come upon bad times. Back at the beginning, grateful citizens wept at the sight of the stars and stripes waving in the free air of a government, of, for, and by the people. Men fought and died for their country and for the high principles for which it stood — but times have changed.

Today there is an ever-increasing number of Americans who are unwilling to pay a price to preserve our glorious heritage. What has happened to us, that we can now stand by and see so many sacred blessings of our forefathers trampled underfoot? Today, ungrateful people, while enjoying the many benefits of the "land of the free, and the home of the brave," work for the destruction of our way of life, the best that has ever existed on this battered old planet.

If anyone had dared to openly despise, insult, and degrade our God-given heritage fifty years ago, they would have been deported so fast it would have taken their breath away. I wonder what would happen if an *Argentine* citizen ever dared to wipe his feet on the Argentine flag, or burn it?

As a layman reads the many and varied explanations for our present financial situation, it leaves his poor mind in a hopeless whirl. It seems as if every "expert" has a different point of view. Whether we call it "inflation" or "depression," it all adds up to the same thing: one awful economic mess! What is the underlying cause? I believe there is one simple answer: HUMAN GREED.

All too many citizens are out for *their* share, *their* rights, *their* benefits. Too many "rights" are adding up to a big fat WRONG. All too few are concerned about the welfare of the country. Padded government contracts are sought by the big time operators, excessive demands are often made by the labor unions, and money-hungry politicians bilk the treasury for themselves and their constituency. Welfare spending has reached astronomical proportions, doled out to almost anybody who comes along, whether there is a legitimate need or not. Greed . . . GREED! What is desperately needed is a huge dose of old-fashioned Holy Ghost repentance! May God grant us a return to the faith of our fathers, and to the Bible they honored!

TOO MANY "RIGHTS" CAN MAKE A WRONG

19

In everything from art to advertising, dishonesty marks our civilization. Campaigners for this cause or that learn how to promote it with clever deceit.

My father, Lawrence B. Saint, was a stained glass artist of some fame; he was also a talented portrait painter, but too honest to please some of his subjects. Once he painted a very handsome businessman; and his wife, in her delight at the result, insisted that Dad paint her portrait too. When she saw the canvas, she was furious, because it showed her exactly as she was, a rather wrinkled, dumpy woman. She refused to pay for it. However, when her son saw it, he laughed aloud, exclaiming, "Exactly like Mom!" — and bought it on the spot!

Today there are social planners who do not paint what they see, but what they want others to see. They picture family life as inferior to government control of children. The housewife, any housewife, is shown as a pitiful drudge, a craven slave, chained to squalling brats and an unfeeling brute of a husband. This worst of all homes is painted as *typical* of most; and a loving father who chastises his child for its own good is portrayed as a "child abuser."

In that, as in much other propaganda, the amount of truth is small. There *are* trapped, frustrated housewives. However, they are but a part of frustrated humanity, caught in its own ugly selfishness. The remedy is not in yanking kids out of the home and into some kind of political commune, but in a spiritual renewing of the hearts of the parents.

Again, the one and only cure is a Person: Jesus Christ, blessing the home with His loving presence. When He is present, the home is transformed. It becomes a place of radiant peace and inexhaustible love. Wifehood with motherhood takes its proper rank as the highest, most fulfilling profession a woman can know.

DEGRADING SOMETHING BEAUTIFUL

21

Are we Americans threatened right now by an alien monstrosity that we have allowed to enter our educational tent? Already an un-elected bureaucracy has become a political dinosaur. A humanistic government-sponsored educational system has moved into our public schools, colleges and universities. Its funds have brought dictatorial control of subjects, textbooks and teaching methods, often in the face of strong parental protest. Talk about overriding people's rights!

When I was a schoolboy, in the assembly period we sang a hymn, had prayer, and somebody read from the Bible. We knew the ten commandments and the Golden Rule. These activities are now forbidden by our country's supreme court, a court which has *not* ruled against depraved homosexual teachers, or against morally damaging reading matter.

What is behind this change? Linked worldwide, certain activist groups are pushing to take control of education at all levels. At the same time, they are openly and severely criticizing the home and all it stands for. They are well financed and are often effective in forming public opinion.

They argue incessantly for more permissiveness in morals, and loudly espouse "new" ethical values (which are really not new, but old and rotten). They have on the drawing board a new world order, with the God of the Bible left out.

They work openly in some places and covertly in others, often using highly respected diploma-bedecked educators and un-elected government bureaucrats.

It would be laughable, if it were not so deadly serious, but they take *our* money in taxes, then offer it back to us as the price of letting them come into our school and family life and take over. With crass arrogance, they tell local authorities, "do as we say, or there will be no government grants!"

These overbearing activists can be checked — but only by determined Christian action. By applying biblical moral principles in the election of worthy political leaders, these insidious and harmful forces can be driven back.

"COME RIGHT IN!"

The ground under our feet trembles to the sinister tread of this man-made monster. With bated breath earth dwellers watch the erratic movements of his menacing, brutal force that is now obviously out of control, heading for a world-wide holocaust.

It is not so much the discovery and development of nuclear power as the awesome fact that it is in the hands of wicked, scheming, aggressive men who do not hesitate to destroy millions of helpless people to satisfy their own insatiable lust for power.

Cloaked under the hypocritical mantle of "detente," and more recently, Salt II, Soviet leaders have been feverishly pushing a continual massive build-up of increasingly refined armaments. When are we going to understand that promises and treaties made by atheists are of no value? Time and time again they have openly displayed their utter disregard for solemn pledges.

When we consider the cruel subjugation in Vietnam, the sufferings of the boat people, the incredibly vicious extermination of the masses in Cambodia, the bloody massacres in Africa, and now, more recently, the openly aggressive invasion of Afghanistan, we are forced to the bitter conclusion that all red pretense of peaceful coexistence is a farce.

God in His divinely inspired Word has forewarned us of the rise, development, and utter annihilation of "Gog and Magog," who will come down into Asia Minor in the last days.[1] Prophetic teachers taught this years ago when Russia was a backward nation of benighted serfs. They sounded a biblical warning of the rise of the "king of the north" long before there was any indication that the inhabitants of the barren, icy steppes would become a world menace.

This colossal, man-created monster is on the loose, as we approach the end of the twentieth century. His ultimate doom is sealed. God will put "hooks in his jaws," and he will fall and be completely destroyed on the mountains of Israel.[2]

[1]Ezekiel 38:2-16   [2]Ezekiel 39:11, Revelation 20:8

MONSTER OUT OF CONTROL

THE STUBBORN CAMEL

HARPING ON ONE STRING

It would be ridiculous, except for the mind-boggling horror that it was built to hide! We're talking about Russia's pretense of "religious freedom." Every bit of it is false, part of the gaudy fabric which is Communist propaganda.

"A murderer from the beginning . . . a liar and the father of it,"* is Christ's description of Satan. It fits the Soviet Union's life history like a glove.

Moscow, a city of millions, has only one church building where a weekly "open meeting" is permitted. Christians are forbidden, on pain of prison or even death, to teach their faith to their own children, young people, or neighbors. Any reported criticism of the Communist regime is punished with brutal severity.

Thousands of authenticated cases, backed by photographs, motion pictures and signed documents verify the macabre methods by which the Soviets suppress religion.

"Jesus to the Communist World," a widely recognized organization, has thousands of cases in its files. These gruesome photos and appalling reports of torture, expose a program of ruthless body and mind control.

Alexander Solzhenitzin, Anatoly Marchenko and George Vins have published detailed reports of the tortures of their fellow prisoners in slave labor camps. By 1967, forty-six new prison camps had been added to the inhuman Soviet system. By 1970 the State-operated radio in Sweden reported "more than three million (Soviet) prisoners, among whom the proportion of Christians is high."

There is a brighter side to these ugly facts: that is the God-given spiritual strength of Christians in countries where the hammer and sickle rule with an iron hand. Their faith is truly "gold tried in the fire." As it was in the early centuries under despotic Caesars, so today, "the blood of the martyrs is the seed of the church."

*John 8:44

BEHIND THE FALSE FRONT

FOLLOWING IN THEIR FOOTSTEPS

THE MEDICINE MAN IS BACK IN TOWN

31

Marxism, as we can see by the picture of two despondent revolutionaries, is parasitic. It is like a leech that can only live by sucking the blood of others. Communist-trained terrorists become experts at destroying buildings and human lives. They talk about their people being all equal, which, by and large, is true — equals in poverty, oppression and slavery.

The Bolshevik revolution in Russia was financed by capitalist American dollars. Leon Trotsky was given a million dollars to underwrite the bloody Marxist takeover of Russia. Bolshevism did not overthrow the Czar. It was overthrown by the Russian peasants and workers. The Communists simply used U.S. dollars to infiltrate and take over by dirty tactics the revolution already won.

It was uncounted tons of lend-lease material shipped by boat to Russia during the war that built up that nation into the mighty war machine that is now a menace to the entire free world; and even today, we are practically giving to Russia all sorts of goods and products that provide the sinews of their war potential.

Communism is like poisonous toadstools that feed on the rotting stump of the capitalistic system. From its early beginnings until now, it has invaded and infiltrated one weaker nation after another, literally sucking the lifeblood from them in order to survive.

In Ezekiel, chapters 38 and 39, we have a clear description of "the king of the north" (that is, north of Palestine) coming down into the Middle East like a swarm of locusts. Gog and Magog mentioned in these chapters have been clearly demonstrated by capable scholars to be Russia with her satellites. Not only does God's prophet describe in detail what will happen, but he tells us what will be the hidden *motive* for this great invasion. It will be to take a spoil, to amass wealth, to take possession of great riches at the navel of the world.

Russia under the grinding heel of Marxist totalitarianism cannot survive without robbing and pillaging constantly. Their insatiable thirst for riches is the motivating force behind their dreams of world conquest.

"COMRADE, I'M BEGINNING TA THINK THAT WE SHOULDNA
BOMBED THAT LAST IMPERIALIST EATIN' JOINT."

What a shock for those who thought "Uncle Sam" was about ready to "shuffle off this mortal coil!" Communistic propaganda has been prophesying the death of our democratic way of life for years; and Krushchev boasted: "We will bury you." But lately there is much evidence to indicate that the patient is doing better, thank you.

It is true that our beloved "uncle" is still plagued by violence and crime, by increasing moral laxity, and un-American socialistic tendencies. Hanging over his head is the continued ominous military build-up of the red world conspiracy — aided and abetted by certain unprincipled financial interests both in Europe and America.

But praise the Lord, there is a massive spiritual awakening sweeping across our land! Coming in fresh from South America, I have seen encouraging signs of a mighty spiritual renewing that is pumping new life into Uncle Sam's tired veins.

In other days, such movings of the Spirit were centered around one man, like Martin Luther, John Calvin, D.L. Moody, or Charles G. Finney. At times, several men were raised up by God simultaneously, like the Wesleys and George Whitfield. But what is taking place today is so vast that no man is seen. The Holy Spirit has anointed a veritable army of leaders; but this rising tide of blessing is much bigger than all the men involved, and goes beyond all human effort. It is worldwide in its scope.

What is happening is not momentary or spasmodic. Prayer groups are being continually held all over the country. Factory workers, high-paid executives, housewives, political figures and military personnel are seeking God in groups large and small. There is no human coordination involved in most of this; but there is a Spirit-implanted pattern that links it all together: free-flowing praise and worship, a warm love that sweeps aside all ecclesiastical barriers, and a solid evangelistic fervor expressed in earnest personal counselling. The similarity between what is happening in the United States and down in Argentina is truly remarkable.

The publishing of books emphasizing the work of the Holy Spirit has been absolutely phenomenal. A pitiful trickle of such works a few years ago has become a mighty river of blessing, as tons of books go out to avid readers everywhere. Sales have exceeded the wildest dreams of Christian publishers. Presses are exhausted from the task of pouring out literally millions of copies of

THE RIGHT MEDICINE WILL HELP A LOT!

power-packed books!

Christian "talk shows" like the 700 Club and the PTL Club are literally covering the entire United States and spilling over into an increasing number of countries overseas. A strong, warm, informal-type witness is going into millions of pagan homes where people never go to church.

Not only so, but Christians are beginning to see that God is backing up the salvation message with answers to prayer for healing and deliverance from mental and spiritual bondage, as the fulness of the Holy Spirit and His gifts are emphasized.

Then there is the return of many thousands of former liberals in our great denominations to an evangelistic thrust, and to a recognition of the charismatic renewal as a work of God in the now.

Outstanding leaders and an increasing multitude of lay people are moving in a new dimension — the dimension of the Holy Spirit. New Testament gifts that have lain dormant for long years have risen like the Phoenix from the ashes of traditionalism.

Pentecostals, long despised and persecuted, are now seen to have been the brave pioneers who have moved out for God in spite of fierce opposition at the outset, back at the turn of the century. Today they are recognized by church leaders as one of the three great mainstreams of Christendom.

Another most encouraging sign of moral and spiritual recovery in the United States is the practical application of Christian principles to the political situation. No longer is the church splendidly (?) isolated in its ivory tower of theological sanctity. Strong opposition is being victoriously raised against pornography, homosexuality, drugs, crime, and irresponsibility in government.

The landslide victory won by President Reagan has demonstrated the powerful clout wielded by awakened Christians. Uncle Sam is not dead yet!

Teen Challenge centers all over the country and overseas, along with Youth With a Mission, Inter Varsity, and many others, are demonstrating that young people are still ready to pay a price to serve Christ their Lord. The tremendous worldwide impact of Wycliffe Bible Translators and the student outreach of Campus Crusades are just part of a global movement of thousands of home and foreign missionary efforts.

So while the enemies of God are surprised to find Uncle Sam doing so well, and are gnashing their teeth in rage, we should rejoice and take heart. Instead of throwing brickbats, we might even take the old boy a bouquet of flowers or a bowl of fruit!

I am convinced that too many of us have been over-influenced by prophets of gloom and doom. Yes, "evil men and seducers shall wax worse and worse."[1] It is true that world slavery is coming, compounded by famines, pestilences, and "wars and rumors of wars."[2] But let us remember that the despotic and diabolical reign of the Antichrist will be only for a short season. *The reign of Jesus Christ, the King of Kings, will be forever!* We are on the victory side! We belong to Him!

Not too long ago I was on a plane flying from Atlanta to Columbia, South Carolina. A fine-looking white-haired southern lady, sitting beside me, noticed my Bible, and we got into conversation. She said that something tremendous had happened to her brother, who I gathered was in his fifties. She told me that for years he had been a typical nominal "Christian," going to church several times a year, as a sort of courtesy call. His life showed no indication of spiritual life or power.

Then another businessman got him to go to some sort of retreat. He came back just walking on air! She said it was truly remarkable. Suddenly his whole life became electrified. He began to go out with a group of men to witness in country churches, home meetings and factories — anywhere the door opened. He was tireless. He seemed twenty years younger.

Then with an apologetic note in her voice, mingled with a bit of concern, she asked, "You don't think there is anything wrong with speaking in tongues, do you?"

I assured her that this was one of the gifts of the Spirit and perfectly okay. She seemed relieved.

This, in miniature, is symptomatic of what is going on all the time, all over our great land. Let's believe God for uncle's full recovery, for the glory of God and the good of the whole world.

[1] 2 Timothy 3:13   [2] Matthew 24:6

When I was a boy in a little country church, we used to sing: "The heathen in his blindness bows down to wood and stone. . . ." Held by my childish limitations, I wondered how the poor benighted savages could be so stupid. Now I understand that idolatry is not limited to ugly idols that look either ferocious or dehydrated.

Our western world is very worshipful. Its big idol is mechanical power based on human intellectual prowess. People operate complicated controls, with humming sounds and flashing lights — power with fantastic ability to delight the body and mind, and also destroy them. In the advanced computer this idol has almost acquired independent life. It threatens to completely dominate us. It is totally heartless and as easily controlled by evil men as by good.

Computerized armaments threaten human existence on this planet. Mechanized industry and mechanical robots concentrate more and more of the world's material wealth in fewer hands. Syndicated entertainment and mind-blowing super movies offer high powered emotional sensations as the best reason for staying alive.

Men continue to be worshipfully dependent on this way of life. They submit themselves to what they themselves have created, instead of to the God who created them. That is their disastrous choice.

God will never take away from man his right to free choice; but in many ways, He warns us of the error of our way, and pleads with us to return to Him, who alone is worthy of our worship and trust.

Today, as ever, Jesus the Lord of heaven and earth stands amid all the confusion and failure of man's best efforts, and says, "Come to me all that labor and are heavy laden; and I will give you rest."[1] And the promise of rest is backed up with another promise, "He that comes to me, I will in no wise cast out."[2]

One of these days our great civilization is going to break down. The awe-inspiring idol of materialism will be found completely impotent. It is high time to put our trust in the living God who created the material universe and us also.

[1]Matthew 11:28   [2]John 6:37

THE GREAT GOD MONEY

TIME

TALENTS

ENERGY

Phil Saint

MODERN IDOLATRY

The cracks beneath him are widening. Nothing can save this ease-loving sleeper unless he wakes up in time. He has been lulled into false security by the creature comforts with which he has surrounded himself.

The dilemma is not only his, but ours; for there is worldwide instability due to crumbling moral standards, and a hopelessly debt-ridden world economy. The planetary food supply diminishes alarmingly. Apocalyptic arms stockpiles reach to the heavens. Earthquakes are increasing, and seismologists predict worse ones in the days to come. World weather patterns are changing unpredictably. Global pollution of air, soil and oceans threatens all living things.

Leaders in science and politics know this; but their carefully measured warnings are swallowed up in the cacophony of mind-seducing, appetite-creating television and magazine advertising. Despair for the survival of our modern civilization is pushed back into the subconscious, but will one day burst forth in world-wide panic.

But here is good news! There is a way of escape from the trembling precipice of world disaster! There is another place of refuge that is secure and eternal — Jesus Christ. The apostle Paul in the Bible declares flatly that, "No man can lay a (permanent) foundation other than the one which is laid, which is Jesus Christ."* The Word of God makes a sharp contrast between the ungodly man who builds his house on the sand, as opposed to the wise man who builds his house on the rock: Christ Jesus.

Divine judgments on a God-rejecting world will appear in greater catastrophes to come. Today there is still time left to heed the storm warnings that are flying along the coasts of today's way of life. It is desperately important for people everywhere to get off the disintegrating shelf of self-indulgence and onto the unshakeable foundation of Christ's kingdom of love.

*1 Corinthians 3:11

ON THE EDGE OF A PRECIPICE

The tired, cynical "old man" at twenty-five, sitting in his broken-down "free love" vehicle, looks with scorn on two young people who have just pledged themselves to one another for life. They are on their honeymoon.

To this jaded character, living with one woman for more than a few weeks or months is unthinkable. He doesn't realize that his so-called "freedom" is nothing but abject slavery to his own base passions and to an implacable master, Satan. What at first seems so exciting soon leads to hopeless life-destroying tangles.

It is like sailing vessels of the last century that became enmeshed in the floating weeds of the Sargossa Sea in the Bermuda Triangle. Gradually the desperate sailors died of starvation and thirst; until finally, a once proud windjammer became a drifting mass of rotting timbers strewn with bleached skeletons of the long-forgotten dead.

Likewise, it is appalling to see how quickly many young people become entangled in a wild round of drinking, carousing, and free-wheeling sex. With what utter abandon they give themselves to the worship of dope-crazed, sex-mad hard rock bands!

On the other hand, the clean, wholesome Scriptural plan for happy married life makes a sharp contrast with the godless filthy living of the worldly crowd. To them, the Bible plan of one man for one woman for life, is slavery. But to Christian young people who love the Lord, it is the only life worth living . . . not for a momentary thrill on a completely selfish basis, but living daily for one another and for God! It is two young people whose great delight is making their partner happy, forming a home where peace and joy reign supreme! It is raising a family of children who will grow up to be a credit to their parents, and an asset to the community. And what is so wonderful about all this, is that it is all for real! God's plan for happy marriage really works! Ask.me, I know — after almost forty years of personal experience.

GOING IN OPPOSITE DIRECTIONS

The little baby mouse is trembling with excitement! His eyes as big as saucers are hypnotized by what he is seeing — a delicious meal prepared just for him! So it is with thrill-seeking adolescents today.

By the millions, they are getting caught in the drug addiction trap around the world.

A number of factors combine to lead them into the trap. In the first place, ours is a hopped-up pleasure-mad environment. Any thought of living a serious, carefully thought-out life, is almost drowned out in a deluge of high-powered advertising that appeals to young people to satisfy their carnal appetites. Live for God? Live for others? Serve humanity? Are you kiddin'? Life is eating all kinds of delicious food, shouting yourself hoarse at a ball game, going to a hotspot to dance, drink, and carouse all night — live it up!

Another factor is the self-centered, hypocritical lifestyle of so many parents. Father tries to curb liquor drinking on the part of his teenagers — while he frequents his private basement bar. Parents can go and wallow in the rottenness of violent crime and perverted sex luridly displayed on the screen; but, oh no! not for tender youngsters under eighteen! Adults take a pious stand against smoking grass — while they themselves are hopeless slaves to nicotine. Daily they demonstrate that their false goals of social and financial ladder-climbing does not satisfy, or produce love and understanding between husband and wife.

So why not smoke grass? And when that palls, why not become a "main-liner"? Old addicts work night and day to enslave others in order to provide themselves with a way to finance their own expensive habit. It is a self-perpetuating evil that slowly but surely tortures its victims to death. Why don't the authorities recognize it for what it is: murder in slow motion? Drug pushers are vicious monsters, and should be dealt with as such. May God help us to break the back of this diabolical attack on our youth!

YOUTH TRAP

The spirit of moral laxity in our modern society is distracting those who have been entrusted with protecting our nation from greedy, unprincipled venders of filth.

Sin has always been with us. From time immemorial, evil men have made merchandise of their fellowmen, providing all kinds of carnal pleasures — for a price.

Ancient pagan kingdoms were riddled with immorality, much of it legalized, like temple prostitution. The sprawling Roman Empire was not conquered by the hordes of barbarians from the north. They destroyed themselves by allowing gluttony, loose sexuality, and violent spectacles in the arena to take over. The barbarians simply moved in and swept up the debris, when the once glorious Roman way of life had become a moral and spiritual shambles.

Fifty years ago, in the United States, most loose living was discreetly kept out of sight. Not any more. Recently I saw an attractive cover in a supermarket magazine rack. Almost without thinking, I reached for it. As I idly flipped several pages, my heart went sick! One full page spread consisted of a colorful photograph so explicit in its seductive appeal that I could not believe what I was seeing.

Vicious peddlers of dirty pornography, vile adult movies, and similar salacious wares, have walked right into our once decent social system. X-rated motion pictures, "massage parlors," and nude girlie bars blatantly advertise their "products" as freely as breakfast foods!

One thing is certain: unless America turns back to God in sincere repentance, and slams the gate shut on open immorality, our nation will shortly be a nightmare of violence and crime — a nightmare from which there will be no awakening. But, praise the Lord, our beloved land can be saved by turning to Jesus Christ, whose blood can cleanse away all sin, and whose resurrection power can put moral fiber into flabby backbones!

DISTRACTED GATEKEEPER

Who in the United States would declare himself against "equal pay for equal work," or deliberately favor underpaying anyone because that person happened to be a woman? Especially we who are Christians and know the Bible are strongly in favor of justice in pay scales and in equitable treatment irrespective of sex.

Even a casual study of the life and teachings of Jesus at once demonstrates His high regard for women. While others of His day ignored or looked down on women, Christ went out of His way to honor them. The first person He revealed Himself to after His resurrection was a woman, Mary Magdalene. He sat and taught one woman, Mary, the sister of Lazarus. He defended the criticized woman who poured out precious ointment on His feet, and wiped them with her hair. He talked with the despised Samaritan woman at the well. In His dying hour, He committed the care of His mother, Mary, to the beloved apostle John. Ordinarily a victim dying on a cruel cross could think of no one but himself. Not so with the Son of God. All through the Bible, we find women whose ability, patriotism and piety were recognized and rewarded.

So here we see Uncle Sam, when faced with the necessity of making a decision, carefully separating the girl ERA from the two "pets" she is bringing. If the supporters of ERA want respectable citizens to endorse their political and social platform, they will have to make a clear-cut break with their pro-abortion plank, and their support of homosexuals.

It has been a matter of grave concern to many, to see nationally influential women identifying themselves with the pro-abortion movement and homos, while at the same time avoiding any relationship with those who are fighting to protect unborn babies from wanton slaughter, or those who are endeavoring to save our youth from the degeneracy of homosexualism.

Let's eliminate unfair discrimination against women, while preserving a wholesome environment for our children and grandchildren!

(THESE) DOGS NOT ALLOWED

49

Suddenly the whole block explodes! Young gang members pour out of alleys in the darkness. Late commuters scurry for shelter. A "rumble"* is on.

What happens to these juvenile thugs who steal, destroy, burn and kill, keeping city dwellers in a constant state of fear and uncertainty? Many times, underage delinquents are given only a few weeks in jail, or a suspended sentence, and let out on parole. Since they are teenagers, we are told that they must be treated with velvet gloves, or slapped on the wrist at sunrise.

The police round them up; but the judges, all too often, let them go because the laws are full of legal loopholes favoring the criminal. Vicious crimes committed by mere youngsters are not dealt with on the same basis as those perpetrated by adults — but the victims are just as dead.

When Noah, in Old Testament times, came out of the ark with his family, God made clear the sacredness of human life and the seriousness of killing another human being. Genesis 9:5 says, "And murder is forbidden. Man-killing animals must die, and any man who murders SHALL BE KILLED." Capital punishment. The reason given for executing the murderer is made clear, "For to kill a man is to kill one made in the image of God."

But some will protest, "Exacting the death penalty is cruel!" Which is more cruel? The killing of the innocent, or the execution of the guilty? If a man wants to avoid being executed, the solution is simple — he must refrain from murdering someone else. The one who destroys the life of another, according to the Bible, forfeits the right to continue living himself. It is that simple. And no exception is made for the killer who happens to be young.

We are paying a terrible price for our permissive treatment of young killers. Human life has become cheap. Television violence has made death commonplace. Human dignity has gone down the drain in a large measure.

*Gang fight

50

IN AGAIN — OUT AGAIN

51

Have you ever noticed how certain people sympathize with the poor condemned criminal and work tirelessly to whip up public sentiment for his release — while the widow and fatherless children of the man killed are completely forgotten?

"The murderer must be pardoned!" After all, he is so young! Only they don't call him a "murderer," but "that poor boy." Some even go so far as to urge that he be allowed to live, so that he can be saved. . . . So we let him out again, and he goes on killing more innocent people. Don't his victims also have a right to live, with the chance of getting saved? It is not a matter of dying or not dying; it is *who* does the dying, the guilty criminal, or his innocent victim?

To justify setting aside the death penalty, defenders of young monsters cry: "Thou shalt not kill!" No clear distinction is made in their thinking between what an *individual* does as a private citizen, and what *the law* does to protect the law-abiding populace. The ten commandments are directed to the individial. "You (as an individual) shall do no murder" (i.e., unauthorized killing).

As Christians, we are to love our enemies. As soulwinners, we are to do all in our power to win criminals to Christ. But as citizens, we must uphold the law, and back those who are commissioned to protect human life. The New Testament teaches in no uncertain terms that the authority of organized government has not been set aside, just because we are living in the age of grace.*

Let us back every effort put forth to bring young criminals to Christ! They desperately need love and compassion. But let us also uphold those who maintain law and order — otherwise our nation is faced with chaos.

*Romans 13:1

ONE-SIDED CONCERN

Discrimination against minorities!" This is the cry of the self-styled defenders of homosexuals. Deceptive propaganda has befouled the issues. The word "discrimination" is now a tar brush, used to blacken any belief, any law, which militates against movements or causes — evil or good.

"Don't pass laws restricting homosexuals — they are a *minority!*" But if we accept that line of reasoning, we must logically apply it to child-abusers, typhoid carriers, and the criminally insane; because homosexuals are akin to all three of these minorities.

The claim made by "gays" (what a misnomer!) that they were born that way, is utterly false for all but a few physically malformed, the hermaphrodites. Homosexual desires, in most cases, are *learned*, and *inflamed* by perverted sex acts.

Some brave Christians have raised the battle flag against the corrupting influence of homosexual teachers in public schools, fighting to deny them access to our impressionable children. If this effort fails, many thousands of our precious little ones will be seduced and enslaved by perverted lusts that wreak havoc among our youth.

The Bible is very clear: "The wrath of God is revealed from heaven against all ungodliness and unrighteousness of men . . . wherefore God also gave them up to uncleanness . . . unto vile affections; for even their women did change the natural use into that which is *against nature:* and likewise the men . . . burned in their lust one toward another. . . . They that commit such things are worthy of death."[1]

Yet for all "gays" there is a way of escape — only one! Jesus Christ. Anyone who has become involved in this enslaving, degrading lifestyle and wants out, can be set free by the all-powerful Savior. Once a victim has fled for refuge to Him; and has made Him Lord of his life, the homosexual or lesbian can say with confidence: "Greater is he that is in me, than he that is in the world!"[2]

[1]Romans 1:18-32   [2]1 John 4:4

DEFENDER OF MINORITIES

How confused can we be? On the one hand we raise a hue and cry about saving endangered species of the animal kingdom — and at the same time kill off millions of human beings before they ever see the light of day.

Isn't it pure insanity to stop the building of a huge power dam to protect a rare three-inch fish, while at the same time doing nothing to stop the cruel murdering of little defenseless people in the womb . . . and they are *people*. Anyone who has seen the heart-wrenching film *The Silent Scream* can never again say that a fetus is a non-human entity to be disposed of as if it were some kind of bothersome tumor. As you see the baby recoiling from and trying to escape the powerful suction tube used in one type of abortion, you can understand that this is nothing but torture and murder.

And why are these millions of little lives snuffed out? In most cases it is simply to avoid the shame of illegitimacy or the bother and expense of caring for a child.

Such degenerates are described in the Bible as being "without natural affection." And the appalling thing is that perpetrators of this crime never seem to think about repenting of their adulterous way of life; nor do they consider waiting until the wedding day before satisfying their sexual desires. Abortion would practically disappear overnight if everyone would reject pre-marital sex and if married people would be faithful to their own life partners.

The murder of innocent babies is not new. It is as old as the ancient Canaanites. Some critics who have never taken the trouble to study into the extermination of the Canaanites by the Israelites accuse the God of the Old Testament of being cruel. He was not. He simply used the Israelites to cut out a deadly moral cancer from the body of the human race. Those pagans were placing their newborn babies on the white-hot arms of the hideous heathen god Moloch and roasting them alive! And if God destroyed the Canaanites for their macabre practices, will He not judge modern nations that are doing practically the same thing?

HORRIBLY DISTORTED PRIORITIES

57

The angel is looking at his watch, or maybe just picking up some cosmic wavelength; but either way, it is time to leave. I'm sure that angels are very patient, since God who sends them is longsuffering and kind. If you were an angel trying to get through to a typical human being, how long would you stick around?

Some spiritual leaders make a big case against television on the basis of pornography, violence and bloodshed, and false concepts of life — and rightly so. But to me, the greatest evil of all is wasting hours and hours of precious God-given time, staring stupidly at the same old stuff on the "boob tube" screen, while the Word of God lies unopened and unread.

Something over two thousand years ago, a distinguished prophet, prime minister of a great world empire, didn't hear from God for twenty-one days; but it was not because he wasn't listening or because his mind was cluttered with a lot of intellectual chaff. It was because powerful demonic opposition delayed the arrival of the angelic messenger. Daniel was in an attitude of constant intercession and expectancy.

However, so many of us today who call ourselves Christians never get the heavenly Word, because we are all too often giving our time and interest to worldly entertainment, creature comforts, and secular pursuits.

Ruth and I, coming up to the States from South America, have been profoundly impressed with the way television, newspapers, magazines, and radio are promising the masses heaven on earth through material things. How many of us Christians, consciously or unconsciously, are allowing ourselves to be convinced that "mammon" (money) can literally provide happiness?

How satisfying it is to know that when we "seek FIRST the kingdom of God and His righteousness," all the things we really need will be added, just as He promised!*

*Matthew 6:33

ANGEL AT THE END OF THE LINE

In desert country I once saw what appeared to be a very real and beautiful shimmering lake surrounded by tall trees. If I had been a thirsty traveler, and lost, I would most certainly have had a strong urge to leave the trail I was following, and pursue the mirage that seemed so inviting.

In the same way, the humanist dream of a man-created Utopia looks like an achievable reality to many very normal people; but it is a deadly deception in the desert of human frustrations, a desert strewn with the sun-bleached relics of past attractive philosophies based on human ability alone.

There is only one way we can survive in the barren wastes of man's fallen nature — follow the map! God has provided a true and dependable map, the Bible. But many who call themselves "Christians" have dropped this divine blueprint, to pursue the ephemeral image of an ideal society created by man's unaided ingenuity.

Where humanistic socialism has been put into practice, the bright illusion is already fading. To those who despair, other mirages beckon: Eastern mystical religions, parapsychology, spiritism, witchcraft — all designed to bring their followers into bondage. Before embracing oriental mysticism, one has only to review the abject poverty, the constant starvation, and spiritual bankruptcy of lands dominated by these Far Eastern cults, to turn from them with horror.

Only in the divine guidebook, the Holy Bible, is there certainty of survival. Thank God, millions today are discovering, or rediscovering, Him who is the "Way, the Truth, and the Life," Jesus Christ.* Only by recognizing the Lordship of Jesus and the authority of the kingdom of God, can individuals or nations hope to find their way back out of the desert of total human failure.

Here in South America, we have been used of God to succor many bewildered souls who have wandered about in the desert of human and Satanic "wisdom," people who have been in and out of mental institutions, who have lost their jobs, and have even become dangerous to themselves and others. To see them sitting in a praise service with shining faces and upraised hands, is reward enough for any teacher of God's Holy Word.

*John 14:6

THE DECEIVING MIRAGE

61

In the hoary year of 1490, ignorance had populated the unknown Atlantic Ocean with fearsome creatures. "Scientists" of that day warned Christopher Columbus that these monsters could gobble up any sailing ship; and if it escaped them, it would plunge over the edge of the world, because, as everybody knew, the world was flat.

Columbus, the great explorer, however, had a firm faith in the face of ridicule that the earth was round and the monsters did not exist — and he discovered America!

Bible-believing Christians today, like Columbus, face "scientific" ignorance of the Word of God.

For the past hundred years or so, humanist philosophy has heaped abuse on the Bible, saying that it is full of monstrous errors and superstitions.

Years ago, I had the inestimable privilege at Wheaton College, of studying under the late Dr. Alexander Grigolia, anthropologist and former atheist, who had worked his intellectual way through the maze of evolutionary half-truths to become a convinced Christian. In the classroom, this brilliant scholar, citing the cold facts dug up by the evolutionists themselves, demonstrated scientifically that the biblical account of creation is correct, and that the various theories of evolution, from Darwin on down, are contrary to the accumulated evidence.

Today, many thoroughly accredited scientists believe that while it is true that there have been wide variations *within* each species, men and dogs, for example, it is also true that each group has been *created* "after its kind."

So we, like Columbus of yesteryear, are not at all disturbed in our faith, by the allegedly scientific assertions that attack the veracity of the Scriptures. We just know that it is time to revise the map.

TIME TO REVISE THE MAP

Pirates of yesteryear, so the reports go, had a simple and gruesome way of eliminating their captives — they made them walk a plank blindfolded, until they stumbled off into the sea. In the spiritual realm, godless educators have taken over many educational institutions founded by godly Christians, and are now imposing their atheistic teachings on impressionable students everywhere.

How many eager young students have left Bible-believing churches and God-honoring homes, only to return four years later, intellectual strangers to their parents who sacrificed to make possible their education! This is the tragedy of modern youth.

On the other hand, there is the good ship "Church and Sunday School" to the rescue! It has sent out lifeboats to save floundering young people from the spiritual despair that would engulf them.

These wonderful Christian schools, founded and financed by generous-hearted parents, are meeting a tremendous need all over the country. While thousands of public school children are menaced by vile pornography and by physical violence in government financed institutions, those who attend Bible-oriented church schools enjoy an environment of order, rapid progress, and spiritual blessing. While state-subsidized public schools are turning out multitudes of semi-illiterates, church schools are producing well-trained future citizens, ready to meet life head-on.

There are those who do not fully appreciate the intrinsic worth of church-sponsored training. For a while, here in Argentina, the Sunday school came under attack from several Bible teachers who taught that the father should be the priest of his family, thereby making the Sunday school unnecessary. The truth is, we need fathers who are priests in their homes, *plus* Sunday school and Christian day schools. The more spiritual instruction the better!

WALKING THE PLANK

Don Quixote, like the Lone Ranger, had many high adventures. But there, all similarity ends. While the Lone Ranger with his brilliant mind and good-hearted spirit always came riding up at just the right moment (thanks to the script writers) to deliver fair maidens and others in distress, Don Quixote, with his few brains addled by reading romantic books about the knights of old, seemed to get himself and others into the most humorous situations — without solving any problems!

So it is with those who endeavor to do battle with the Bible, the Word of God. Mistakenly thinking that the Bible is a collection of superstitious fables that needs to be destroyed, atheistic scientists ride forth to conquer this spiritual windmill, that to them, seems like an evil giant. They, too, suffer ignominious defeat.

The great French infidel Voltaire, with typical humanistic arrogance, prophesied that a hundred years after his death, the Bible would be a forgotten book. He no doubt gave himself the credit for this promised defeat of the Scriptures. However, his clever and cynical attacks against the Bible were overthrown; and a hundred years after his death, they were printing Bibles on his own printing press.

The United Bible Society alone printed in 1979, 259,000,000 Bibles and Testaments; and Ken Taylor's marvelous *Living Bible* has gone to 25,000,000 copies at this writing.

When a blacksmith, whose daily task was to shoe horses, was asked how many anvils had been worn out by pounding on them year in and year out with hammer blows, he replied, "The anvil wears the hammers out, you know."

For thousands of years, the enemies of God's truth have pounded away at the "grand old Book," and the blacksmith shop of time is strewn with piles of worn out atheistic hammers. Meanwhile, the great anvil which is the Word of God, lives on, blessing untold lives and influencing the course of history. Yes, Don Quixote rides again — and meets the same ignominious fate.

DON QUIXOTE RIDES AGAIN!

This interesting African hunting technique serves admirably to illustrate what the spiritistic cults are doing to capture and enslave the unwary. The clever hunter bobs and weaves in the tall grass, causing the dummy head and neck fastened to his head to simulate the movements of another ostrich. In the same way, modern cult leaders often use a pretense of "science" to cover up the same old occult practices of spirit mediums, witches, and oriental gurus. Ostentatiously, they offer new psychic breakthroughs which they call "extrasensory perception" and "parapsychology"; but behind the scenes they are working to bring people into bondage. The pot of "mind control" is waiting for the unsuspecting victim.

Maria M——, petite mother of five husky children, fell victim to the occult. She and her husband were invited by relatives to attend "scientific lectures" on parapsychology. It sounded very intellectual. In the first six conferences, apparently learned professors talked exclusively of the findings of modern science in regard to extrasensory perception.

Then they were invited to a theatre meeting. They expected more of the same, but were surprised to find the auditorium darkened except for psychodelic lights that cast a weird red glow over the platform. A witch-like woman disappeared behind curtains to get in touch with the unseen world.

Suddenly Maria became overpowered by a terrible fear. Moments later, she leaped to her feet, scrambled to the aisle, and fled outside, followed by her distraught husband. From that moment on, Maria was dominated by fear — fear of evil spirits, fear of a curse put on them by "those people," fear of being alone, and fear of being with people. She became afraid of strangling on food and refused to eat. Soon her body had wasted away. A doctor told her that unless she ate and took her medicine she would die. She sullenly refused, held by occult powers.

Then God in a wonderful way brought her to Lake Valley. There, surrounded by warm-hearted praying Christians, she began to eat. In no time she accepted Christ, and became a radiant believer, a model wife and mother. Christ saved her from physical, mental and spiritual ruin!

STALKING THE PREY

A small boy was picked up, broken and dying at the foot of a quarry. His superman cape was torn and bloody. He had gone back into the field at the top of the precipice, and running as fast as his little legs would carry him, had leaped out into space. His last words in the hospital were: "I almost did fly like superman, until I landed at the bottom . . ." Blood filling his lungs and bronchial tubes, strangled further comments. Power, *power*, and more POWER, is what Satan is offering people in our day. Not only physical power, but mental and extrasensory power — the "wisdom of the ages."

And just as Eve in the garden of Eden fell for Satan's subtle offer, "You shall be as gods," so today, many are becoming enmeshed in the devil's web of lies, through his offer of power. It is a deceptive and lucrative puppet show that is capturing the attention and enlisting the cooperation of untold thousands in our modern world.

It was the promise of power to build an ideal social order, that drew unsuspecting victims after the diabolically clever Jim Jones. Some nine hundred fanatical followers and fearful victims either committed suicide or were forced to drink cyanide-spiked punch. The exciting puppet show put on by this alleged Christian minister-turned-Marxist, had done its evil work.

Jim Jones is gone; but multitudes of others have picked up the puppets of "power" and "wisdom" and are continuing to deceive gullible people.

Is there no alternative? Yes there is — Jesus Christ, who said, "All power is given to me in heaven and earth," and who offers us the divine wisdom of the Word of God and the Holy Spirit. The power and wisdom of Satan lead downward to destruction. They enslave and mutilate their victims. The power of the Gospel of Christ and the wisdom of the Sacred Scriptures set us free to walk in newness of life. This is no make-believe, no puppet show. It is the real thing!

THE PUPPET SHOW

God's Word cannot be silenced, but it can be obscured. So Satan jams the divine airwaves, knowing that confusion does the trick as well as anything.

Our civilization is constantly bombarded by appeals and directives from every quarter. The truth-seeking pilgrim feels helpless, and strangely alone. Often in desperation he follows one or another sign, only to find himself at a dead end. "There is a way that *seems* right to a man, but in the end, it leads to death."*

Jesus saw the people of His day as bewildered sheep without a shepherd, so the Bible says, "He began to teach them many things." He is still doing this, through the written Word, the Bible — and through us. He commanded us to go and "teach all nations." In order to do this, we must somehow get them past all the man-made signboards, so that they can see for themselves what the Word of God has to say to them.

"Science says . . ." "The cults teach . . ." "Your horoscope indicates . . ." "Reason declares . . ." Then, too, some appeal to plain common sense; and, of course, many quote the pronouncements of human-endorsed church traditions.

But what people desperately need in these days of confusing voices, is to hear the clear voice of God as it is in the sacred Scriptures! Jesus spoke with authority, and not as the scribes and Pharisees of his day. He never said, "We may well suppose," or "It might be true that. . ." or "I'm not sure, but the latest reports indicate . . ." Jesus our Lord spoke with *divine authority!* And we should speak in His Name, with all the authority of His Holy Word.

The bewildered traveler here shown reads that the Son of God died for " . . . what?" Praise God, the rest of the message clearly states that He did not die for truth. He did not die for His teachings, or His cause — He died for *our sins* according to the Scriptures!

*Proverbs 14:12

TOO MANY BILLBOARDS

I believe that many of those who see this cartoon will agree with me that something demonic is being perpetrated on the masses today by means of deliberate distortion of the facts about life in general and Christian truth in particular. Godless propaganda is being spewed forth recklessly by vicious criminal-bent beasts whose only interest is in raking in the shekels and lining their pockets with gold.

When a promoter learned that a whole new chain of multiple movie houses was being built in a certain large city, he exclaimed to the big-time operator of the grandiose project, "But there are already enough theaters available for the few good films coming out!"

The cynical reply was, "That's right, but we are not interested in showing 'good' films; the weird, the occult, the violent and dirty films are the in thing." He paused; "This is what the public wants to see today, and this is where the big money is."

Today, anything goes, ANYTHING! These degenerate vendors of pornography, sexual perversion and violence do not hesitate to lay their filthy hands on the most sacred themes. Theatrical productions and so-called "sacred" films are now portraying Christ as the poor, weak victim of His own stupidity — while picturing Judas as the smart one who saw the situation back then as it really was. Christ, all biblical information to the contrary, is shown variously as a homo, Mary Magdalene's lover, and the vacillating dupe of His ephemeral ideals that could never be realized.

To soup up their corrupt presentation, they do not shrink from having naked women dancing around the cross, while others are engaging in sexual posturing and violence.

The most shameful aspect of all this is that these productions are shown and performed in so-called "Christian" churches as well as in theaters.

Behind all this there are evil forces marshaled, not only to make big money at the box office, but to destroy the moral fiber of all mankind. Satan is known as the destroyer. Jesus called him a liar and a murderer; and that is exactly what he is.

THE DIABOLICAL BILLBOARD AD

Africa's Serengeti Plain, where rhinos and lions roam, is a safe place — compared with the savage spiritual jungle in which you and I actually live. Fiendish murders are common front-page news; and there are satanic cults, witches' covens, "spiritist" seances, and tons of books on witchcraft and the occult. Then there are the related mind-traps of parapsychology, mind therapy, and oriental rites.

The only people who can bring down the mighty rhinos of demonic power are those who know how to use the high-powered rifle of God's Word.

A Christian minister of my acquaintance answered a knock on his door, and found himself face-to-face with just such an enemy. The young man standing there invited him outside, and then in the street, said: "I am a priest of the church of Satan. When I raise my hand, a strong wind will blow down this street."

He did so, and the sudden gust came. He dropped his hand and the wind ceased. "Can your master show such power?" he asked.

My Christian brother answered, "Yes, Christ has *all* power in heaven and earth."[1] After giving an earnest testimony about God's *spiritual* power, as opposed to mere *natural phenomenon*, he invited the young man into his house; and there, through the next several days, the ex-priest of Satan remained on his knees before the open Bible, crying out to God in heaven for mercy. He found that the high-powered weapon of the Word of God stopped the demonic forces in his life dead in their tracks.

The Bible states: "Our struggle is not against flesh and blood, but against . . . spiritual forces of wickedness."[2] The mad beasts of the unseen world are no match for the Holy Scriptures. Even Christ Himself, when tempted of the devil in the wilderness, three times defeated him, saying: "It is written"![3]

[1]Matthew 28:28   [2]Ephesians 6:12   [3]Matthew 4

BIG GAME HUNTER

Can you *feel* the joy of this old miner? He has struck it rich after years of unrealized hopes, unrewarded labor. He has found the wealth of his dreams, and knows just where to get more.

The precious ore was put there by God for anybody; but it has to be found by somebody who is willing to dig it out. My father was a rich man — in the gold that God has stored in the Holy Bible. He was determined to show us children what it looked like, and where to find it. Then it would be up to each one of us to roll up our sleeves and dig it out.

Dad promised each one of us kids ten dollars (which was a big sum back in those days) for each time we'd read the Bible through. I read it from cover to cover four times before I was fifteen; although I must confess that I skipped over the long chapters of "begats"!

Dad's life glowed with a spiritual wealth that we couldn't help seeing all our growing years. I know that I soaked up some of this, inevitably, through the pores of my skin, if not through head and heart! It built into me a wholesome aversion toward dishonesty, wrong sex, profanity, and the like. It gave me a hunger for the "unsearchable riches of Christ."[1] That hunger led me to dig up the true gold of God's eternal Word; and the desire to share this "Good News" led me into the ministry.

Today, as I build my sermons, I am constantly amazed to find that I can recall just the verses I need to emphasize what I want to teach. This is the work of the same Holy Spirit who revealed His riches to my dad.

Yes, "thar's gold in them thar hills" — for you, too! It is there for the taking. Your labor, reading God's Word, will be rewarded by "treasures in heaven,"[2] that you can begin to enjoy now.

[1]Ephesians 3:8   [2]Matthew 6:20

"THAR'S GOLD IN THEM THAR HILLS!"

How awful it must be to feel alone in this vast universe — no Heavenly Father who knows, loves or cares! No absolute truth, no intrinsic beauty, for all, to the atheist is only relative.

Since he has persuaded himself that both the universe and he himself "happened by chance," he can have no real goal, no destiny. He is just a chance-assembled machine. He can only obey impulses and seek sensations.

Christ is ever near, standing in the shadows, ready and willing to be his Divine Companion, Guide and Deliverer; but the humanistic materialist doesn't see spiritual realities. Why? Because the "god of this age has blinded the minds of unbelievers."[1] The atheist's blindness condemns him to an existence without meaning, and a death without hope.[2]

About 3,000 years ago, David, the royal prophet, declared, "The fool has said in his heart, there is no God."[3] You see, the real trouble with the atheist is not intellectual, but moral and spiritual. Thus, the Psalmist goes on to say, "Corrupt are they; their deeds are vile . . ."[3]

It is logical to believe in Jesus Christ. If we can't believe in this One who so clearly demonstrated His deity — who *can* we believe in? Unbelief is really only a cover-up for a rebellious, morally distorted life. I once debated a long time with a storekeeper in Chile. He tried to prove that the Bible was full of errors, and that there was no God. It was all very intellectual. Later I learned that he had deserted his wife and was living in adultery with her sister.

We whose eyes have been opened to see Jesus, the Light of the world, know that our loving Creator cares for each of us, as if we were the only being in the entire universe.

[1]2 Corinthians 4:4   [2]Ephesians 2:12   [3]Psalm 14:1

BLIND BY CHOICE

81

Sitting on the floor, legs crossed, head bowed, eyes closed, muttering over and over a secret word called "mantra" — this is the usual plan for relaxing your nerves, getting your body tone in shape, and eliminating the cobwebs from the old gray matter. It all appears to be so practical and so necessary in a world that seems to be more and more uptight as the days go by. The main thing is to let the mind go blank; and very few who follow this procedure realize, until it is too late, that when the mind is thus conditioned, it is easy for evil spirits to take over. And they do, in many cases. Victims of these oriental cults start with what they think is innocent psychological therapy — and end up offering flowers before the picture of a defunct guru, which is really an act of submission and *worship*. The guru may be dead; but the unclean spirits are very much alive.

Christian meditation *is* transcendental, since it has to do with getting in touch with Someone higher, and beyond ourselves. We, too, endeavor to get quiet before our God; but we do not let our minds go blank, nor do we indulge in "vain repetition as the heathen do." Praise the Lord, we keep our minds full to overflowing with the glorious light of the Word of God. We ponder Spirit-given verses of the Bible. Meanwhile our hearts are full of Jesus and His wonderful love, a light that is so dazzling that satanic demons are forced to flee!

Across the years, not only the Bible itself, but deeply spiritual teachers have emphasized the "quiet time," "getting alone with God," and "listening to His voice." All this is true transcendental meditation; it is moving into the realm of the Spirit.

A famous poet once said, "The world is too much with us, late and soon," a quaint, old-fashioned way of saying, "It's time to split."

Let's refuse to clutter up our minds with meaningless drivel and downright crut! That may mean an implacable monitoring of television programs and reading material. Let's keep that heavenly light blazing away in our minds and hearts!

MEDITATION THAT IS REALLY TRANSCENDENTAL

83

Boom towns of the far west are mostly gone. But all too many modern churches are carrying on the same desire to make an exaggerated impression on the general public. Unnecessarily expensive, lavishly-adorned buildings are defended (in a world of hunger and poverty) as a means of attracting the unchurched. If this is the way it is to be done, why did not Christ our Lord and his disciples do it? Should the people of the world be drawn to Christianity by this all-out appeal to the senses — or challenged to a life of sacrifice and service in a world of desperate need?

The worst of it is, that all too often, behind impressive buildings and programs, there is concealed an appalling spiritual poverty. High decibel music is relied upon to attract carnally-minded worldlings, like flies to honey. A shallow, easy-believism offers instant formulas for entering the kingdom of God. No embarrassing questions are asked about unconfessed sin in the life. A real, scriptural repentance is carefully avoided. Just say the right words, and you are in!

Our Lord Jesus taught otherwise. He said, "If any man will come after me, let him *deny himself*, and take up *his cross* daily, and follow me."[1] There is no eternal life without this commitment. Yes, salvation is absolutely free. Jesus paid the complete price for our redemption. However, to receive this free gift, and to identify with Christ, we must be willing to pay a price, and that price is to die to self, so as to live unto God.

If the Apostle Paul had the idea of appealing to people through a demonstration of earthly splendor, there is no sign of it in his inspired writings. He said flatly, "I am *crucified* with Christ." Crucifixion is *death*, death to carnal desires and human approval. He went on, "Nevertheless I LIVE! yet not I, but CHRIST LIVES IN ME!"[2]

I personally believe in attractive functional buildings designed to hold people, a lot of people. I am convinced that a Spirit-led program needs no carnal embellishments to draw people to Christ. He said, "I, if I be lifted up from the earth, shall draw all men unto me."[3]

[1]Luke 9:23   [2]Galatians 2:20   [3]John 12:32

BOOM TOWN FACADE

85

A new nature! That is what we receive when Christ comes into our lives as Lord and Savior. In a moment of time, we lose our appetite for the "dump heaps" and the "garbage" of this world.

Our twin sons were never drug addicts or dissolute, but they were rebellious for several years, partly because I was not the father I should have been. They wanted no more church, no more Bible or prayer or sharing in God's work. Joe seemed the more hardened of the two. Their mother and I grieved; but one night, the Lord gave me a vivid dream of Joe, kneeling by my bed, weeping over his sins and accepting Jesus as His Savior. Ruth and I took courage, and began to give thanks in advance, for what we knew He was going to do.

A year later, the twins reached their moment of truth. At that time they were with us at the Lake Valley Conference Center — but only as truck drivers and helpers around the grounds. They studiously avoided spiritual matters. However, one night, Joe had a long serious talk with Susy (who is now his wife). Later, sitting alone by the well in the darkness, as the pump poured water into one of the swimming pools, the Lord met him.

Moments later, I opened my eyes in the middle of the night to see our Joe kneeling by my bedside, exactly as I had seen him in my dream a year before.

"Oh, Dad, Mom," he burst out. "Jesus is real! Jesus is real!"

Meanwhile, his brother Jim had been spending long hours in earnest conversation with Lynn, another Spirit-filled girl. At the close of a meeting, he rushed to the platform and gave me a bear hug that nearly cracked my ribs! He watered my shirt with his happy tears; because he, too, had become a new creature in Christ, with a completely new appetite. In that moment, "old things passed away, and all things became new."[1]

Yes, you guessed it, Jim married Lynn, and both couples are now enjoying the lush green pastures of God's blessings.

[1]2 Corinthians 5:17

HE LOST HIS APPETITE

Our perspiring friend has had it! He has been working feverishly, and, as he sees it — well. The dragon's long leathery tail is neatly tied down, as its owner looks on with mild interest, a bit baffled by what he is seeing.

Much of the preaching I heard in my teens was a sincere but misguided effort to tie the dragon's tail — a series of "don'ts." Don't swear, don't drink, don't gamble, don't smoke or dance. By avoiding these manifest evils, we were supposed to be instant examples of what a good little Christian should be. *Inner attitudes*, it seemed to me, were seldom mentioned.

Of course, this negative approach cannot really immobilize the dragon that lurks in the human heart. Jesus said, "Out of the heart come evil thoughts, murders, adulteries, thefts, false witness, slanders."[1] He exposed the hypocrisy of the scribes and Pharisees of his day who were wholly concerned with *outward* forms of godliness. Jesus scathingly condemned them, saying: "You clean the outside of the cup . . . but inside you are full of robbery and self-indulgence . . . false pretense and lawlessness."[2]

Praise God, Spirit-filled preachers are now boldly, if belatedly, dealing with wrong *inner* attitudes: fear, hate, pride, self-seeking, jealousy — internal manifestations of the dragon that destroys so many souls.

How many of us were spiritually defeated, fighting to control external behavior patterns, until we were filled with the Spirit of God Himself? In my own life, since receiving the infilling of the Holy Spirit, outward words, outward behavior, and my relationships with others have notably changed.

The victory over overt actions is won down deep inside. When the inner complexes and hang-ups are forthrightly dealt with, the actions other people see are automatically brought under control. "But thanks be to God who *gives* us the VICTORY through our Lord Jesus Christ His Son!"[3]

[1]Matthew 15:19   [2]Matthew 23:25   [3]1 Corinthians 15:57

TYING THE DRAGON'S TAIL

There he goes on his wild chase after "success," "acceptance," and "fame"! The throttle is wide open! The motor is roaring! Waves are foaming wildly as they fan out behind — GREAT! But there are huge rocks on every side, some just under the surface, waiting to tear the bottom right off the boat and sink it to the bottom. But father is having a delightful time proving that he is a big he-man who knows his way around. . . .

What is so tragic about all this is that he has with him a very special group of captive passengers: his own family. Whether they like it or not, whether they agree with his craze for high-speed living or not, they are caught, bound by family ties that most of the time they cannot break.

Leave it to the kids to see through the sham and hypocrisy of parents who are on a wild ego trip. Father or mother may think they are fooling the neighbors and the gang at the office; but the kids live behind the scenes, and they know all about the two-faced sham going on — Dad's smiles and polite words before strangers and acquaintances, followed by glowering looks and bitter words when the alien spectators have safely gone.

How much of what we adults do is not so much for our family as for ourselves? How often we are terribly upset about our rebellious children, not so much because we are concerned for *their* future welfare, but because the way they live reflects on *our* good name? Ask me, I know. It was not until I stopped worrying about how the rebellion of our twins was affecting *my* reputation as a missionary and Bible teacher, that they began to change. When they saw that (finally!) I was really burdened for their spiritual and temporal welfare, they began to soften, and reconsider their anti-religious way of life. When at last, I realized that their indifference to my wishes was simply a reflection of my own indifference to my Heavenly Father's will, the tide began to turn.

Praise be to God, my family is no longer a captive crew, forced to put up with my blundering around! Believe me, this pilot now guides his family boat with great care, past the jutting rocks that menace our spiritual safety!

CAPTIVE PASSENGERS

91

There he is, snorting ferociously, stomping and bucking, the uncontrollable beast fabricated by our own carnal nature! The tongue. God's description of this small but all-important member of our bodies, as described in the book of James, is a scorcher. After giving us a long list of the evils of the tongue, God says it is "set on fire of hell."[1] He starts out with a flat statement: "The tongue can no man tame."[2] Gossip, bitter criticism, and exaggerated rumors have destroyed more churches, more families, and more individual lives, possibly, than any other one factor. Relatively insignificant actions have been blown up into a federal case. A moment of weakness in an otherwise beautiful Christian life has been taken out of context, distorted, and made to say that white is black, and good is evil.

And so this vicious homemade rampaging bronco, called the tongue, continues to ruin good reputations, drive honest businessmen to bankruptcy, break up happy marriages, and damn young lives to futility and failure.

How easy it is to jump to wrong conclusions, and criticize others unmercifully! With shame, I have to admit that for many years, my besetting sin has been the tendency to downgrade others in order to upgrade my own supposed importance and success. I could see the faults of others, magnified by my own pride and self-confidence, as glaring weaknesses that needed to be pointed out. I did not realize that this strong inclination on my part was clear evidence of my own insecurity and fear in the face of my own spiritual weakness.

My father told me that one time he arrived late at a meeting, when the visiting preacher was already into his sermon. Dad felt critical of God's messenger, on seeing that he was leaning on one elbow while preaching. Shame filled my father's heart, when, at the end of the Bible message, the pastor turned and hobbled back to his pulpit chair — he had only one leg. Praise God, He can tame our tongues as we turn them completely over to Him!

[1]James 3:6   [2]James 3:8

92

ON THE RAMPAGE

Across the centuries our Captain's call rings out: "FIGHT THE GOOD FIGHT OF FAITH!"[1] But there lies the snoring, lazy Christian! His "helmet of salvation" is perched on the bedpost; the mighty "Sword of the Spirit, which is the Word of God," hangs listlessly, unused. His "shield of faith" serves no real purpose because he is asleep.

The command of our Commanding General is very specific. He says, "Put on the whole armor of God, so that when the evil day comes, you may be able to stand your ground."[2]

Today, under Marxist regimes, faithful Christians meet secretly for worship, Bible study and fellowship. When caught, they are often beaten, imprisoned, even killed; but their daily life has a divine joy and vitality seldom seen among ease-loving churchgoers in the so-called free world. God's armor for those suffering persecution is not for parade-ground antics. Like the apostle Paul, they have scars from their many battles with satanic hosts. They are "more than conquerors through Him that loved [them]."[3]

Until I was twenty-one, I was a lazy Christian. Oh yes, I was busy in the church, using up a lot of "animal heat." I sang in the choir, took up the collection, and worked in youth meetings; but as far as any real, earnest battling with the Enemy was concerned, I was practically worthless.

Thank God, all that changed when Dr. Albert Hughes, fiery Canadian Bible teacher, thundered out on the text: "I will show him how great things he must suffer for my name's sake."[4] Weeping for shame, I knelt at the altar, and sobbed out to the Lord: "If you will keep me busy, I will serve you till I die." That night I put on the armor, and have been on the battlefield for Christ ever since, by His grace.

[1] 1 Timothy 6:12   [2] Ephesians 6:12   [3] Romans 8:37   [4] Acts 9:16

IT'S NO KNIGHTGOWN

When I was a skinny peewee Boy Scout, I sometimes wondered if I'd ever make it to the end of that long hike in the hot sun. Then, with money earned from selling newspapers in our country town, I bought my first binoculars. They really changed my viewpoint. If I looked through the wrong end, what I wanted to see was impossibly distant; but if through the right end, I was almost there!

Weak faith always looks through the wrong end. God's promised *abundant life* seems utterly unobtainable. Fear of failure saps our will to even try. Prayer languishes, spiritual work sags to a new low — and Satan cackles with fiendish glee. It is he who many times, without our knowing it, reverses our mental and spiritual binoculars, to throw us into hopeless confusion.

Sometimes he suggests that, as sinners, we are not worthy to receive anything from the Lord. But remember, the devil is "a liar and the father of lies."* Anyone who has welcomed Jesus Christ into his life has become a child of God. As an accepted member of the divine family of heaven, redeemed and forgiven, we *are* worthy both to ask and to receive. Our Father above lovingly waits for us to ask Him for all we need.

Studying ornithology at Wheaton College, I learned that certain birds, such as the eagle, can turn on instant telescopic vision. Through the use of an amazing organic optical device called the "pecten," these high-flying birds can see sharp details on the ground — when a man below can barely see the birds soaring like a tiny speck in the sky.

Then there are owls that can see clearly in the dark, where we would be stumbling about blindly. God will give you and me, as born-again members of His family, power to turn on the instant telescopic vision of spiritual discernment, bringing both Him and His blessings "closer than breathing, and nearer than hands or feet." This is the supernatural power of living faith. Ask for it! Use it! . . . and whatever you do, never look through the wrong end of the binoculars!

*John 8:44

LOOKING THROUGH THE WRONG END

Who hasn't been there at some time or another in his life — bogged down in an apparently hopeless financial mess? I certainly have; and as I look back on a number of heartbreaking experiences, it reminds me of something that took place in Japan when three of us were holding meetings and distributing Scriptures with the Pocket Testament League. We travelled to hundreds of cities and villages, after the war, from Tokyo, everywhere south.

One day, on a dirt road, we were assaulted by a drumming downpour of rain. At a certain place we had to cross a rice field on what had quickly become like sun-melted chocolate. We slithered into the ditch. The panel truck tilted at a crazy angle, up to the floor boards in oozy gumbo mud.

After a while, a huge charcoal-burning Japanese truck came lumbering along. In no time, they had a long cable tied to our rear bumper, and had pulled us out with smiles and bowing all around!

I have gotten myself into a number of financial mud holes, with every day a desperate struggle to get out of the red. At first, I usually blamed unexpected circumstances that were beyond my control; but later, I came to see that I had just bitten off more than I could chew. I had made no allowances for the unexpected that always shows up sooner or later.

The Bible says that each man must bear his own burden.[1] The important thing is for us to find out just exactly how much, and what sort of a load the Holy Spirit wants us to carry. All too many times we add personal projects to what God gives us to carry.

Of course, we call this "faith"; but sometimes it is sheer presumption. The Word says bluntly, "Owe no man anything but love."[2] Nothing could be clearer.

At times, we are just not willing to wait. What we want may be good — but not for right now. Adjusting ourselves to God's timing is tremendously important.

May the Lord help us to keep out of the bogs and swamps of debt — and stay out! Let's breeze along on the highway of freedom from the crushing burden of unmet obligations!

[1]Galatians 6:5   [2]Romans 13:8

BOGGED DOWN

Satan has built high, strong walls to keep his enslaved people from the knowledge of God.

On the other hand, God's warriors, working together, power the battering ram of unceasing united prayer — and down come the walls! Great cracks appear; building blocks of demonic lies fly in all directions. The oppressed captives of his empire of darkness get a look at the truth, and many escape through the broken walls to the "liberty for which Christ has set us free."[1] And notice that the battering ram of united prayer also protects those who are inside it from "all the flaming arrows of the evil one."[2]

It was prayer plus faith, led by trumpet blasts, which caused the flattening of the walls of Jericho.[3] Unceasing intercession during the days before Pentecost was the effective preparation for the glorious moment when there came the sound of a "mighty rushing wind . . . and they were all filled with the Holy Spirit,"[4] and three thousand people from all over the Roman empire were rescued from the "dominion of darkness, and brought into the kingdom of the Son He loves."[5]

When the Bible says that the Gospel is the "power of God,"[6] it uses the Greek word for "dynamite." We can go one step further, and declare that it is more powerful than the neutron bomb!

In preaching the invincible message of Christ over many years, I have seen all kinds of imposing walls come down — but never without earnest spiritual warfare (knee action) on the part of the body of Christ.

In Argentina over a period of years, we have seen people come to Christ in great tent campaigns and at our Bible conference center. Souls have been saved, and there has been a good measure of growth in the body of Christ throughout the country.

But now, just recently, great walls of pride and prejudice have crumbled and come down as Christians have cried out to God. We are seeing today a spiritual breakthrough such as we have never known before! Satan's hold over the minds of the masses has been loosed, and multiplied thousands are turning to God!

[1]Galatians 5:1   [2]Ephesians 6:16   [3]Joshua 6:20   [4]Acts 2:24   [5]Colossians 1:13
[6]Romans 1:16

. . . AND DOWN COME THE WALLS!

The case of the sacred cows of India has been used to illustrate many untouchable situations. Here I am using it in relation to our denominational structures which all too often hinder the unity of the body of Christ. Many denominations have programs so highly organized that there is no room for interdenominational activities. The Holy Spirit is hindered in demonstrating that we are really *one* in Christ. All too often, we emphasize our special doctrinal differences to such an extent that the basic oneness of Christians is lost in the shuffle. I am not talking about apostate religionists; I am talking about born-again believers.

One good brother whose doctrinal position does not allow for fellowship with a number of other evangelical groups once said to me, "Well, we will all be one in heaven."

I replied, "But Christ prayed that we all might be one, THAT THE WORLD MAY BELIEVE."* It is clear that Jesus prayed for unity among us *in the now*.

In some parts of India, if a cow decides to take a little siesta right in the middle of the tracks, the trolleys just have to wait until his highness decides to move on! Nobody pokes the sacred animal. And it would seem that many Christian leaders have the same attitude toward their denominational structures. It has become a form of idolatry for some. Their denomination is more important than the Word of God. As one leader admitted, "Yes, what you teach is biblical; but it is not according to the doctrinal position of our church."

It is high time that we put the true, invisible church in its proper place, subordinating everything else to it. When we are more loyal to our sect than to the whole body of Christ, we are blocking the way to the uniting of the body worldwide.

As a bandit once said to his henchman, "If we don't hang together, we will hang separately." Perhaps this is a far-fetched example for Christians; but if we would "hang together," we would really be a powerful testimony to the world.

*John 17:21

THE SACRED COW

I recall the day, early in my ministry, when I built a sectarian snowman. I rudely turned my back on a brother in Christ, and marched out of his house. He was an older, more experienced and more gracious Christian than I. We had been planning some work together for the Lord — until he told me the startling thing that had happened to him in answer to prayer. The Holy Spirit had suddenly flooded him with such love and praise to God that he was like a drunken man for the next three days.[1]

In the teachings of my church such "emotionalism" could not possibly be of God. So I picked up my notebooks and drawings and left.

But by the mercy of the Lord that was not the end of the matter. That dear couple prayed for me for about thirty years; and at last Jesus' love melted away my cold prejudice — even dried up the puddle of its melted water! My experience with the Holy Spirit was different from his in its outward manifestations; but the breaking up of the spiritual ice pack and the outflowing of divine love were the same.

A snowman is not only cold; it is lifeless. It can be dressed up to look real (in a dim light), but it lacks the one proof of reality, *living warmth.* So it is with all our denominational pride and prejudice.

It is not so much the *denomination* that is wrong; it is *our attitude* toward it that causes so much trouble in the body of Christ. Just as we have families with different names, so we can have church families with different names. In one family there are people with various personalities and a variety of viewpoints. But when we get puffed up about our great denomination — and look down upon those of other sectarian groups, the coldness gets into the marrow of the bones, and the body of Christ is seriously weakened.

Among the disciples of Christ there were James and John "the sons of thunder," there was impulsive, blabber mouth Peter, and quiet, studious doctor Luke; yet they all loved and obeyed one leader: Christ their Lord. Together with sound doctrine, there must be love, divine love that fills us all, crossing all denominational lines.[2]

[1]Acts 2:15   [2]1 Corinthians 13

MELTING SNOWMAN

From the desert country of the old Southwest, to the sawdust arena of Madison Square Garden, cowboys have captured the imagination of America! Just the mention of a *rodeo*, and the world of young people begins to boil with excitement! When the powerfully muscled steer breaks out of the chute with a cowboy in hot pursuit on his fast mustang, everybody holds his breath. How many seconds will it take him to rope and tie his elusive quarry?

But there is a wild bull that defies all man's attempts to stop him. It is our own carnal nature that refuses to bow to our earnest desires to subdue him. How many times have we said: "I'm not going to lose my temper anymore"? But what happens? Before we know it — zass! There we go again! How often have men sworn that they are through with liquor, or other women? But that old fallen nature refuses to be roped and thrown, and the awful slide to hopeless defeat continues. The same is true of drugs, and a long list of other evils.

But there is one cowboy who can bring any outlaw nature into submission — Holy Spirit fulness. Christ said, "It is expedient for you that I go away."* Why? "Because," He affirmed, "if I go not away, the Comforter will not come to you." He sent the Holy Spirit down to take His place, and to make Him and His teachings real to us. The Holy Spirit, through the power, wisdom, and love He imparts, can rope, throw, and immobilize this rebellious nature of ours. And He is the only One who can do it.

The first time I saw cowboys roping yearlings in the corrals of New Mexico, I was absolutely astounded at the way those wiry sons of the plains, together with their magnificent horses, could bring down those unruly beasts in seconds. Listen, that isn't anything compared to the skill of the Holy Spirit in conquering these stubborn carnal natures of ours!

*John 16:7

106

ROPING THE WILD BULL

In the province of Cordoba, we welcome the rainy season, as they did in the Near East, where the Bible was written. In Palestine, the "early and latter rains"[1] brought abundant crops from the soil and much joy to the hearts of the people. At harvest time they had a special thanksgiving festival marked by singing and feasting.

Today around the world, Christians are experiencing a downpour, the promised "latter rain" from God. Peter on the day of Pentecost spoke of the time when God would "pour out His Spirit on all flesh."[2] He linked it to his day and to ours.

As the abundant downpour blesses the church, the truth sprouts and grows, pushing up through the formerly dry ground of "churchianity." All over the world, renewed believers are forgetting their denominational differences. The hard clods of bitterness and jealousy are softening. Love and understanding are preparing the way for a great harvest of souls.

When Youth With a Mission came here to the world championship soccer matches to tell of Christ's mighty saving power, they were amazed at the Argentines' eagerness to hear them, especially the young people. Government paid interpreters even went so far as to translate their testimonies from English, French and German, into Spanish. God had prepared the soil through the gentle rain of the Holy Spirit.

Many New Testament passages indicate that what began at Pentecost was meant to continue right down to the coming of Christ. Jesus said very clearly that the power the disciples would receive was for testimony "both in Jerusalem, in all Judea, Samaria, and to the ends of the earth."[3] This clearly includes us, since He also said, in the Great Commission, that He would be with us alway, "even to the end of the AGE."[4]

[1]Joel 2:23   [2]Acts 2:17   [3]Acts 1:8   [4]Matthew 28:20

"HERE IT COMES!"

One morning, here in Argentina, I awoke with the basic idea of this cartoon full blown. The Lord, I believe, gave it to me. It proved to be the birthday of a series of cartoons, as the Holy Spirit resurrected a long-forgotten talent, and put it to use.

Back in my childhood, as a gangling, freckle-faced country boy, I had dreamed of becoming a great cartoonist. Herbert Johnson, then staff artist for the *Saturday Evening Post,* lived just two miles up the road from Huntingdon Valley, Pennsylvania, where I grew up. Whenever I caught a glimpse of this distinguished, white-haired cartoonist driving through our sleepy little hamlet, my heart leaped with excitement! Someday, I, barefoot Tom Sawyer-type, would be rich and famous, and own a big shiny car like that! Little did I imagine that God had very different plans for my life, like drawing with chalks to illustrate Bible truths on the platform both at home and abroad.

So during forty-five years of evangelistic campaigns, all thought of drawing pen and ink cartoons for publication was thrust into the background. Then, recently, it was as if the Lord pressed an unseen button and said, "Now you are ready."

It was amazing to me to see, how in my sunset years, my early training under Herbert Johnson came back to me, and the varied factors involved in producing cartoons just seemed to fall into place. I'm sure, also, that the patient, love-motivated teaching of my father, a very talented stained glass artist, had much to do with these drawings now being published.

YES, THE TIDE IS RISING, AND IT IS TIME TO CUT THE ROPE! Today the muddy flats of spiritual stagnation, strewn with the old tires, tin cans, and rubbish of human traditions are disappearing in many places. Boats of Christian service, once stranded, and lying helplessly on their sides, are now floating gracefully!

My big problem in the face of this beautiful change, was that I had been saturated for many years with teachings on the *negative* aspects of the endtime apostasy; you know, the "Antichrist," the "great tribulation," the "lukewarm church," and so on. But thanks be to God, the marvelous infilling of the Holy Spirit prepared me for the massive *positive* renewal that the Lord is now sending upon the whole world. It provided the spiritual solution I so desperately needed — and didn't know it!

Like so many, I had been thoroughly programmed against "Pentecostalism." Strong mental blocks had been fed into my

A SIMPLE SOLUTION

"computer" against what my Bible teachers declared to be "false doctrine" coupled with "shallow emotionalism." So I clung tenaciously to what I considered to be "sound doctrine," until clear Bible truths cut me loose.

It all began when our son David, dissatisfied with the uninspired, if not boring, meetings at our local church, became interested in going to Pentecostal services. Ruth and I were so anxious to "protect" our oldest son, then in his late teens, from what we considered to be rabid religious disorder, that we prevailed on him to go to a good fundamental Bible institute in Buenos Aires, over 500 miles from Cordoba, where we lived.

When he came home on vacation, we noticed a big change in his life. He spent much time in his room on his knees in prayer; and he was always grabbing his Bible and going off in search of his unsaved pals.

One day we had a little prayer meeting in our bedroom. Ruth and I were kneeling beside the bed, heads bowed and eyes closed. I had finished praying, and while Ruth was taking up where I had left off, I heard David murmuring along at the same time! I thought to myself, "Why, that's strange; we always pray one *after* another." So I stole a glance. David was standing at the foot of the bed, his face uplifted, hands raised to about the height of his shoulders. There was a wonderful expression on his face. He was obviously in close communion with his Lord.

I listened for a moment. "Why, that isn't English; and it sure isn't Spanish!" I was piously shocked! I thought, "Oh, Pentecostalism has penetrated our good Baptist home!"

So I decided to straighten David out — right then. Guess who straightened out whom? The amazing thing was that when I jumped him, David didn't get nervous or uptight. I didn't know it then, but this was one of the many blessings of the baptism with the Holy Spirit. He just said quietly, "Dad, we have accepted without question a lot of teaching against the so-called 'sign gifts,' such as healing, tongues, and visions, without ever really studying the matter carefully for ourselves."

There is a lot more to be told about my subsequent spiritual pilgrimage; but this was the beginning of a theological earthquake that shook my neat doctrinal structure to its very foundations, and led me step by step to a thorn tree in a sun-bathed valley in the mountains of central Argentina. On that epoch-making day in

1967, under that humble tree, I cut the rope that bound me — that invisible man-made bond that for so many years had kept me from moving on for God. A national pastor, at my request, laid hands on me, and I received what Jesus Himself called the "baptism with the Spirit," and I began to pray in a beautiful language I had never learned.

That was just the beginning of living in a new dimension for me. I knew that I had been indwelt by the Holy Spirit and that my body was a temple of the Spirit since my conversion as a child; but this was an infilling and outpouring to provide me with power for witnessing like I had never known before.

Cutting the rope that ties a boat to the dock may seem like a trivial thing; but when I severed the spiritual ties that bound me to a limited ministry, my life boat began to move out into the powerful current of the love of God that carried me into a flow of God that I had not known in other days. Various gifts of the Spirit that had lain dormant for so long sprang into life. I experienced a wonderful peace and joy I had not known before. Frustrations and hang-ups began to melt away. I began to get along better with other people. The guidance of the Holy Spirit became clearer, and I made far fewer mistakes in judgment than in former times.

Instead of being all wrapped up in my "great" projects, I found myself listening to the problems and heartaches of others. I began to pray for the sick, and many of them were healed. God granted me encouraging visions in moments of great trial that lifted my spirits and calmed my fears.

It is not that I felt myself to be better than others; it is just that I knew that I was far more blessed than before this thrilling experience. I am now more aware of how unworthy and useless I am, while at the same time enjoying an anointing and power that is new and wonderful every day. How thankful I am that I cut the rope!

The rising tide of Holy Spirit blessing, while making possible an exhilarating journey to the full Gospel dimension, can really be rough at the outset. It creates new problems for the comfortable dispensational Christian. It was so in my case. Our financial support, as missionaries on the foreign field, came from brothers in Christ who were, for the most part, dead set against anything that smacked of emotionalism. As far as they were concerned, I had "gone overboard." And it was true in a very real sense — but not in the way they thought! I had gone overboard like a scuba diver who revels in plumbing the depths of the sea.

This new spiritual experience with the Holy Spirit had provided me with the means of reaching thrilling new depths of glorious adventure in Christ; and soon I began discovering fabulous treasures in the Word of God that I had never seen before. They had been there all the time, of course; but until I got "all wet," I did not and could not take advantage of the "sign" gifts of the Holy Spirit, which are available to the church today.

At first, I decided to keep my exciting discovery to myself, and not tell my home-front friends what was going on in my life. But God saw to it that my unwillingness to speak out was dealt with. Some missionaries felt it necessary to inform our supporters that we had departed from accepted dispensational truth, and had gotten into error.

Then two young ladies who had come all the way from Brazil to spend several weeks at our summer Bible conference center, returned to report that we were running a program with all the fixins', hand clapping, amens, the works. This shocking news was flashed to our fundamentalist constituency in the States. Immediately a letter came to my desk in Argentina, the first of many similar letters to follow: "I hear you are all mixed up in this tongues business. We are cutting off your monthly support."

I wrote back that I was not "mixed up," but straightened out. I patiently explained that one who believed that the baptism with the Spirit and *all* the gifts of the Spirit were for today, was more fundamental than those who declared that the so-called "sign" gifts had passed away. My reply fell on deaf ears. They had already made their decision without giving me an opportunity to explain what I now believed, or why.

114

THE SCUBA DIVER

Our missionary support dropped off alarmingly; so I came back to the States alone for a tour of meetings. My first week at a large summer Bible conference was abruptly cancelled. Others went through with the scheduled and advertised meetings, then quietly dropped us.

Since almost no one on the charismatic-Pentecostal side had heard what was happening, we suddenly found ourselves in a vacuum. But our trust was in the Lord; and great joy filled our hearts, knowing that we were in the will of God, and on the right track.

Soon new doors began to open. At a Full Gospel Business Men's luncheon, we had a time of prayer. One of the men, Bertus Koehler, of Paterson, New Jersey, suddenly spoke up.

"Brother Phil," he said, "I see a man coming to you. . . ." I thought to myself, alarmed, "He *sees* a man?"

He went on, "He has his hands full of money for Argentina." He paused for a moment, as if trying to see more clearly, then said, "I'm not sure, but he looks like a Latin." I thought he had taken leave of his senses!

But within a month, a medical specialist whom I scarcely knew started sending in big checks that not only kept us as a family alive, but carried forward the construction program at the Bible conference center in Argentina. God had raised up *one* man to replace many who had cut off our support.

Praise the Lord, the vision was very evidently from God, and was fulfilled; but, I said to myself, "He isn't a Latin." Later, I discovered that this good doctor is French, and French are Latins!

Since that time, our missionary support has come back steadily. In spite of dire prophecies of doom about our future, many new and wonderful doors have opened to us, and the work has grown beautifully. That first week in the United States, I met Dan Malachuk of Logos International, and the book *Amazing Saints* was born. It tells the story of God's gracious dealings with us as a family, up to and beyond the moment when we donned our spiritual diving equipment, and began to explore the treasure-strewn depths of Christs' full salvation.

Now, almost every day, something happens to let us know that Jesus our Lord is with us in a very special way. He was with us in a limited measure before we acquired our full Gospel diving equipment; but it has all been greatly intensified and filled to overflowing with glory since then! Yes, we really have gone overboard, but it has all been to the good; and many serious problems have been marvelously dealt with, through getting down to where the treasure trove of God's complete salvation is.

In other days, I had the answer to the sin question, offering forgiveness to all through the precious blood of Christ shed on the cross. I had the answer to spiritual death through the new birth and could assure unbelievers of a place in heaven beyond this life by trusting Jesus.

However, I had no real answers for those who suffered from demonic oppression or victims of cancer or other serious ailments. I had neither faith nor divine authority in such cases. But all that changed when I dove down to the depths of God's love and discovered rich, spiritual treasures of His marvelous grace.

Not long ago, the daughter of a man with cancer called me on the phone. She had brought him to Cordoba, our city, to put him in the hospital. Before coming, she got in touch with friends in Rosario, asking for the name and phone number of someone in Cordoba who could visit and pray for her father. They gave her my name.

When I arrived at the hospital, the daughter met me: "The doctors have told me that the biopsies showed that the cancer has spread throughout my father's body and that no operation will be any use."

Assuring her that God can go beyond anything that medical science can do, I went with her to the ward where the old man was located. I found that both he and his daughter were Pentecostal Christians who believed in God's power to heal. After encouraging him in the Lord, I called for oil and anointed him with the laying on of hands. I felt the presence of the Holy Spirit very strongly.

The next night, when I met the daughter in the corridor, she said that when the nurse had come in the morning to siphon off accumulated liquid in his lungs, she was amazed to find none. During the day, his swollen stomach went down to normal. Two days later he was dressed and walking up and down the hall!

With his eyes sparkling and a big smile on his face, he said, "Praise the Lord, I'm going home tomorrow!" Two weeks later I had another phone call from the daughter: "Dad is back home, feeling just great — the Lord healed him completely!"

Like the happy little bear cub, today's teens no longer have to make do with the dry roots, the grubs and grasshoppers of uninspired church activities. They're finding the love, joy and peace of a living God, in free-flowing worship, glorious music, warm communication, and the Holy Spirit's supply of tasty gifts and delicious fruits, which never run out!

Not long ago, Ruth and I were in two meetings in a traditional church. We had not been in services like this for some time (not because of unwillingness on our part, but for lack of invitations from the traditional groups). We were saddened to see the serious lack of spiritual flowing. It was all so mechanical, so desert-dry! The singing of random choruses in a superficial way cried out for more sugar and less powder-dry spiritual food.

In sharp contrast was a morning worship service in the Huntingdon Valley Presbyterian Church I had attended from the age of seven through my teens. In those early days, the church was a little white box on a country hill, with a long shed at the back for the horse-and-buggy transportation that brought country people in from the farms around about. Now it is a large complex of cut stone in a thickly populated area of suburban Philadelphia — and now filled with a renewed congregation.

I entered with pastor Bill Groff, wearing the prescribed black robe (something most unusual for me!). The format of the service was typically formal; but there, all suggestion of mere ecclesiastical routine ended. There was *life* in the singing of both choir and congregation. The full-throated organ, under the inspired touch of Mrs. Edwin Flack, leaped into glorious harmonies, filling the sanctuary with joyful sound. (Beverly has played the organ in that church since we were both in high school together.) When we sang the grand old hymn *We're Marching to Zion*, we felt as if we were already in heaven!

Not only teenagers, but all of us, can say with the fuzzy little bear cub, "Oh, WOW!"

THE HAPPY LITTLE BEAR CUB

119

In Bible times, God's people worshipped Him with joy that could be heard! Psalm 27:6 proclaims: "At his tabernacle will I sacrifice with shouts of joy; I will sing and make music to the Lord." Psalm 47 begins: "Clap your hands all you nations; shout to God with cries of joy." Sounds a bit noisy, doesn't it?

So it is with those of us who proclaim the full Gospel; it is done joyously! Where there is joy, souls are saved, churches are revived, people experience healing, and lives are set free from the power of demons.

Who objects? People who *ought* to join the voices raised in praise and thanksgiving. Why do they object? Most often because they've been taught that *all* religious expression should be subdued, "dignified," unemotional. But this contradicts the Bible! The Inspired Word tells us to *"shout* with joy to God, all the earth! Sing to the glory of His Name!"[1]

The little tugboat, alive with Holy Spirit power, is pulling an amazing load. It is noisy by nature. Its booming sound that reverberates up and down the river warns: "Make way for God!"

In our mixed-up world there is far too much meaningless noise, in entertainment, and even in some religious circles; *but it pulls no load.* The Scriptures refer to it as "sounding brass and clanging cymbals."[2] This kind of disorderly sound is not to be confused with "joy in the God of salvation."

Jesus Himself stood in the court of the temple and cried with a *loud* voice: "If any man thirst, let him come to me and drink. Whoever believes in me, as the Scripture has said, streams of living water will flow from within him."[3]

Our Savior is still calling. His complete Gospel, like a powerful tugboat, is towing more churches and more people than ever, through this world's troubled waters — and there is joy in the sound of it!

[1]Psalm 66:1, 2   [2]1 Corinthians 13:1   [3]John 7:37

120

THE SOUND OF ACCOMPLISHMENT

There is an old saying, "Birds of a feather flock together." This is not only true of birds — it is true of people. We have a strong natural tendency to fellowship with those who "see eye-to-eye with us." It is easier and more comfortable. Many of us have never developed a vision wide enough to include the whole body of Christ. We draw lines and raise barriers between ourselves and others who have different views on secondary doctrinal points. Here Dr. Owl, the traditionalist, takes upon himself the task of admonishing another "bird" who happens to display feathers of another color and form. This tendency is all too common between members of different denominations; and at times, discussion of these minor differences becomes a bit caustic. And sharp criticism is not all one-sided by any means!

It is imperative that we emphasize the points on which we agree, down-playing other matters that are not really as important as we make them. We all, fundamentalists, charismatics, and Pentecostals, insist that the Bible is the Word of God, that salvation is by the new birth, through the death of Christ on the cross. We all believe in the Person and work of the Holy Spirit. The second coming of Christ is one of our cardinal beliefs, along with the reality of heaven and hell. We agree on the basics. We recognize that there is really one true mystical church, although in practice, we often fail to demonstrate this oneness before the world.

In the light of the fact that Jesus said, in the great commission, "They shall lay hands on the sick, and they shall recover,"[1] should we make a big issue of the laying on of hands? And since the apostle Paul by inspiration of the Holy Spirit, said, " . . . And forbid not to speak in tongues,"[2] does anyone have the right to forbid others to speak in tongues, if they do it scripturally? Paul, the apostle to the Gentiles, writing to Timothy, said, "I will therefore that men pray every where, lifting up holy hands . . ."[3] So why should anyone label this as a Pentecostal practice, and censor who ever does it? The same with clapping hands and other biblical practices.

This is not to say that everybody *has* to do all these things; but it is an appeal to all of us to refrain from imposing our personal interpretations of Scripture on others who have clear teachings to back up what they are doing.

[1]Mark 16:18   [2]1 Corinthians 14:39   [3]1 Timothy 2:8

TROUBLE IN EDEN

A well-known renewed leader suggested that it might be good if a way could be found to put newly Spirit-baptized believers in a straitjacket for six months until the first waves of overwhelming joy and blessing have subsided! What he meant, I'm sure, is that this tremendous experience all too often leads to ill-advised testifying and impetuous action.

Those of us who have revelled in the surging tides of Holy Spirit outpouring can well understand those who let their newfound experience run away with them; but there is a real need to learn *how* to share what God has so graciously given us.

The talkative parrot pictured here is doing just what he really doesn't want to do — running off the very one he wants to win over to his side.

"Yackety yak, yackety yak." One mistake we often make is in discounting all that the Lord did in our lives *before* we received the baptism with the Spirit. A little sober reflection will reveal the fact that God *did* bless us back then, up to the point of our Christian experience at that time.

In my case the Lord used me as an evangelist and many souls were saved before I opened up my heart and mind to Holy Spirit fullness. Once while I was waiting for a bus on a street corner in Cordoba, a young man jumped off a bus of another line that had stopped to pick up passengers. He ran over to where I was standing, threw his arms around me and told me he had found Christ years ago in one of my tent campaigns. Then he jumped back on the bus as it pulled away and disappeared!

I believe it is important to keep balanced and not go to extremes. Those who oppose the operation of some of the gifts of the Spirit often seem to be obsessed with tongues speaking. This is *not* a "tongues movement." It is not confined to Pentecostals. We must avoid an unwarranted emphasis on tongues and healing. We honor those who faithfully teach the Word of God even though they may not go along with us on tongues and healing as being for today. All the gifts are important; but more important is the love, joy, peace and power that flows out to others as a result of the fullness of the Holy Spirit in our lives.

ANOTHER KIND OF TONGUE MOVEMENT

Over the years I was warned to avoid anybody who claimed a special Holy Spirit baptism. These offbeat people were pictured as "odd-balls" given to erratic emotional girations. Their weird behavior was said to be spiritually ruinous and very contagious.

For half a lifetime I never questioned this caricature, for it was generally accepted by "wise" Bible-believing preachers. Their description seemed very real, especially since I never had any close personal contact with these allegedly unstable and misled types. How could I know that I was looking at a distorted image?

Then some fourteen years ago I began to examine the facts regarding the baptism with the Spirit. Finally convinced, I came into vital contact with Spirit-baptized Christians, instead of just their twisted reflection. I discovered that while there are some wild, far-out mystics (at times, even under definite satanic influences), the *great majority* of true Bible-believing Spirit-baptized people are beautiful examples of the early disciples of Jesus after their transforming upper room experience. Where the Spirit *flows*, the life *glows!*

What a great day it will be for the church, when we all take the time to sort out the facts about other groups from the blown-up, twisted caricatures foisted off on us by the devil himself! How I praise God that I am no longer seeing my Spirit-filled brethren in a distorted mirror!

When a non-Pentecostal pastor, in conversation with me, began "landing in" on the Pentecostals, I politely interrupted him.

"You may be interested to know," I said, "that I, and the great majority of Pentecostals and charismatics, are just as much against 'wildfire' as you are." I hope I was able to get his eyes off the distorted image, and to begin to contemplate the many sincere, earnest, intelligent Spirit-baptized Christians there are around.

IT DEPENDS ON WHERE YOU LOOK

While on a tour of missionary rallies, Ruth and I traveled in a beautiful van, generously loaned to us by a true friend of missionary outreach. It was a lifesaver for the two of us, who were not as young as we had been. Instead of arriving at meetings worn out and beat up, we reached our destinations rested and ready for action. We never would have held up under the wear and tear of 16,000 miles of road travel (not counting plane mileage) for seven months, if it hadn't been for this blessed vehicle.

So we are in no sense against a reasonable measure of comfort and attractiveness in the church buildings that are really dedicated to the glory of God. Many unsaved attend church for the first time, not for the message so much as for the air conditioning, the lovely music, and the modern style of the building.

But, as missionaries who have seen the tremendous physical and spiritual need of so many in underprivileged nations, our hearts ache when we see millions of dollars spent on *unnecessary* luxury items that belie the message of Christ about self-denial and care for others in their need. Too many times the foreign missions program is like a little beat-up bug car on a tow bar behind an extravagantly luxurious microbus with all sorts of glittering extras.

We down here in South America are absolutely convinced that God wants His great commission to be completed — and SOON! That is why we left the shores of our beloved homeland, and came to live and work in Argentina. We don't believe that missions should be an afterthought in local church planning.

How our hearts were lifted when we arrived at the Tabernacle Church in Melbourne, Florida, and saw a large but simple auditorium designed for comfort and utility, without man-glorifying flourishes. Jamie Buckingham and the good people who meet there know that it is not necessary to impress the people of the world with outward show — if the power of the Holy Spirit is freely working within!

Bob Smith, pastor of the fast-growing Parkway Christian Fellowship, calculates that they may well have saved nearly half a million dollars by choosing a functional-economical type of structure, which, by the way, is just as attractive as any ornate building. What is supremely important, he says, is the flowing of the love of Christ inside.

ON THE TOW BAR

Millions of people around the world, especially those who eke out a bare subsistence in poverty-stricken lands, see a great difference between the lowly Man of Galilee and many of those in favored nations who claim to be His followers.

I am not the only missionary who returns to the States and finds himself overwhelmed with the feeling that many Christians are so wrapped up in buying this and buying that that they don't really see those millions out there who seldom if ever have enough to eat, who are without medical aid, without education, and above all, without the Word of God.

It is not my business to sit in judgment on my brethren in Christ. Each of us will have to give an account of himself to the Lord.[1] But I do have an obligation as a faithful servant of Christ, to point up the prevalence of the "me-first" way of life of many who claim to be following the Lord Jesus Christ.

My twenty-odd years as a missionary in South America have given me a revised concept of wealth. I know now that any family with access to good diet, decent clothing, and a safe shelter from bad weather is "rich." A family that has a bathroom and a well-stocked kitchen is "wealthy." If it owns a motor vehicle of any kind, it is living like "royalty."

We *are* royalty. As the old song puts it, "My Father is rich in houses and lands; He holdeth the wealth of the world in His hands." In a very real sense, "all things are ours in Christ."[1] I believe God wants us to have the modest comforts of life. Our Lord told us to "seek first the kingdom of God and His righteousness."[2] But He didn't stop there. He said, "And all these things (food, clothing, shelter) will be added unto you."

But why does the Lord often give to His children *more* than they need for themselves? Is it not in order to give to those who are less fortunate than we are? Praise the Lord for the multitudes of unselfish, truly loving Christians who are not "passing 'buy' on the other side."[3] but are giving of themselves and their money to meet the urgent needs of those who lie bleeding and broken along the road of life!

[1] 1 Timothy 6:17   [2] Matthew 6:33   [3] Luke 10:31, 32

PASSING "BUY" ON THE OTHER SIDE

FISH THAT EAT FISH

THE MODERN TITANIC

THE FANATICS

BEHIND THE VELVET CURTAIN

The story of *Gulliver's Travels* has delighted four generations of children and adults. To Jonathan Swift, its author, the tiny inhabitants of Lilliput meant people of every age who are confined to one or two small islands of tradition. These "tiny" folk see any man of larger vision as a foreign giant threatening their fragile, traditional structures. Before he knows it, they will have bound the unwelcome invader, head, hand and foot, with meticulous care. To their dismay, he wakes up — to burst their little cords like spider silk.

It is really a funny picture. Nothing and no one can tie down Truth's immensity for long!

If we see Gulliver as representing the full Gospel view, we can understand why the Lilliputians of the partial Gospel want to immobilize him. They are afraid — with good reason — that the free-striding man-mountain will crush some of the orderly theological buildings among which they always felt so safe.

Growing acceptance of the whole New Testament's message, including its crisis experience with the Holy Spirit of Truth, is bursting the thread-like bonds of Lilliput; i.e., traditional prejudice, sectarian strife, racial discrimination, and denial that the sign gifts are still the church's heritage.

As Ruth and I have crisscrossed the United States on our missionary tours of meetings, we have rejoiced to see so many "old-line" Christians awakening to the new thing God is doing these days. Many thousands of believers are beginning to "believe *all* that the prophets have spoken," as the Lord Himself opens up their minds and hearts to the outpouring of the Holy Spirit. We have seen the Gulliver-church waking up, and it is a thrilling sight!

LITTLE PEOPLE ON THE RUN

Once, as I was driving through a suburban area, I heard a loud police whistle. I stopped abruptly. Sitting on the curb, almost completely hidden by a large officer's hat, was a small boy entertaining himself by blasting away on his father's whistle — enjoying the nervous reaction of drivers passing by! Relieved, I drove on, my hair gradually settling back into place!

Such a childish pastime is innocuous enough; but in the spiritual realm, it can be tragic. The Bible is clear. It says: "The pastor must not be a new Christian, because he might be proud of being chosen so soon."[1] He must learn to follow before he is allowed to lead.

A young missionary came to Argentina armed with his college and seminary diplomas. He was to work with a veteran national pastor who had founded more than twenty-five churches and had led thousands to Christ. The young missionary, completely ignoring the older man's long years of experience, moved in and took over. With a fine disregard for his own serious language handicap, and his almost total ignorance of the people and their customs, he began making major policy decisions. It was a disaster for all involved.

In Florida some years ago, I had a meeting in a lovely home. Instead of the usual forty or fifty happy, praising believers, only about ten showed up. A young "shepherd" had gone all over ordering people not to attend because the head of that home had not felt led to submit to him.

The Bible doesn't say that we are to order *others* to submit to *us*. It says: "Submit *yourselves* one to another in love."[2] So let's keep in mind that it is God who exalts leaders in His own time and way.[3]

[1] 1 Timothy 3:6   [2] Ephesians 5:21   [3] Daniel 2:21

TOO MUCH, TOO SOON

Across the centuries God has laid His hand on some very unlikely people, from our standpoint, to engage in spiritual building construction. He took William Carey, an English shoemaker, and plumped him down in the heart of India. He chose Smith Wigglesworth, a humble, practically illiterate plumber, to reveal deep truths of His Word to thousands. He found a tall, gangling country boy in North Carolina, whose great obsession was playing baseball, and made him an evangelist to millions, Billy Graham.

In every case, knowledge and ability were combined with Holy Spirit outpouring. Here in Argentina, I learned a lot about building construction. Never in my wildest moments did I dream that God would call me to supervise such an undertaking. By nature I am the most unbusinesslike person that could be found. But little by little the Lord began training me to direct the creating of a Bible conference center that now has twenty buildings on a large piece of property.

Construction work here, due to the scarcity of lumber, is almost all brick, stone, and cement. The valley was strewn with loose stones. At first I was frustrated because of this "oversight" on God's part; but soon I realized that He had put all those rocks there to go into the foundations and walls of the buildings. On every side we found tons of sand and gravel, free for the taking. Brick kilns were smoking along the road nearby. We were in business.

But the one element that put it all together was endless gallons of water. So it is in the spiritual realm. Christ spoke of a fountain of living water, springing up within us — the Holy Spirit. Filling the heads of new Christians with information, even biblical information, means nothing without the anointing of the Spirit. It is possible to stuff people's heads with doctrines, facts, etc., without ever getting the job done for God. So let's not forget the water — the fulness of the Holy Spirit.

THE PERFECT MIXTURE

For many years my father designed stained glass windows for beautiful cathedrals; so I often saw the stone cutters at work. Rough blocks of rock were brought from the quarry to the shops. There they were carefully shaped to the space allotted to them by skilled architects. No stone ever went directly from the quarry into the wall. There was the tedious process of cutting away what was superfluous and straightening out that which was crooked.

It is the same with the spiritual building of God, called the church. For years we have endeavored to bypass the divine process, ignoring the heaven-sent blueprint. But things are changing. Now wise master builders are shaping lives before fitting them into the invisible but very real structure of the church.

How prone we have been in times past to shove uncut, shapeless lives into the walls of the visible church! So-and-so is a prominent member of the community, and besides, he has piles of money. We will elect him treasurer of the church, and hopefully, when he sees a deficit, he will dig down in his own pocket and foot the bill. . . . No matter that he is unspiritual, short-tempered, or worldly-minded — in he goes!

Mrs. Socialite has a gift of gab, is very efficient, wears stunning clothes, and has a lot of friends. We will appoint her head of a Sunday school department.

But by the present gracious moving of the Holy Spirit, countless lives are coming under the sweet discipline of the Word of God and the Holy Spirit! Thousands of formerly rough-cut, undisciplined believers are submitting ourselves to the, at times, painful cutting process that God has ordained — and we are being formed into living stones. It takes time, but the results are just wonderful. Let's all allow the Lord to "shape us up!"

THERE ARE NO SHORTCUTS

When we find ourselves snarled in a welter of tangled traffic during the rush hour, we might do well to recall the early days of the bone-shaking covered wagons, with no well-cushioned radial tires, no automatic shift or power brakes!

Here I have endeavored to capture the thrill of the renewed church, joyfully leaving spiritual dryness behind and rattling happily on to the blessed end-time harvest. The two galloping horses that make this possible are "evangelism" and "Biblical discipleship," an unbeatable team!

Some Christians put such strong emphasis on evangelism that they forget the tremendous importance of Scriptural discipleship, which, by the way, is not some sort of military dictatorship. Thus, for the moment, during a special campaign, there is great excitement! Hundreds of "converts" are counted; thousands are stirred to a sudden spurt of evangelistic effort. But it is clear from the aftermath that all too much of our big deal evangelism is more "animal heat," than Spirit-empowered ministry. At times, worldly-minded "personal workers" are signed up, whose main virtue is the ability to learn a prescribed "soul-winning" approach to those who come forward.

However, in spite of organizational failings, we all know that thousands have been definitely saved in evangelistic efforts large and small. Praise the Lord!

On the other hand, some leaders become completely absorbed with their own already saved clique. One "prophet" in South America even went to the extreme of saying that God was not interested (today) in the salvation of the lost, but only in the perfection of the saints.

He is interested, totally interested in *both*. Christ's disciples, while learning from Him, were constantly winning the lost. They stayed in the upper room only long enough to receive power to go out and win thousands to Christ.

Evangelism, to be truly Scriptural, must be closely linked with follow-up discipline; and discipleship must never lose sight of the Lord's command to "go into all the world and preach the Gospel to every creature."*

*Matthew 28:19

LEAVING THE BADLANDS BEHIND

145

Satan's strategy has always been, "Divide and rule." He uses man's inherent pride, prejudice, fear and hate, to cause endless divisions, setting husband against wife, children against parents, workers against employers, nation against nation, and members of one race against another.

Christ's love brings all different kinds of people together in love, the "squares," the "diamond-shaped," and the "triangular."

At the first Bible conference, where I worked as a waiter, I came to know and love a black chef and his wife who were wonderful Christians. One day when we were in the kitchen together, "Big Tom" told me how he and his wife had gone for a stroll on a beach along the southern coast. This was long years before the present acceptance of blacks in the United States.

Without realizing it, they wandered onto a "white" beach, and suddenly found themselves followed by several burly young whites. Knowing of cases where blacks had been assaulted, and even killed, with the criminals going scot free, Tom and his wife turned and hurried back the way they had come. Just as the growing volume of four-letter insults indicated that the attackers were ready to strike, another powerfully built white man came up alongside.

In a low voice he said, "Just keep walking. If they lay a finger on you, I'll tear them to shreds!" Later, when the young punks had gone, he told them how, when he lay wounded on a battlefield in France, abandoned by wildly retreating buddies, two black men, risking their own lives, had stopped to carry him to safety.

"I have always been grateful," he said with a friendly smile.

This is what happens when God's love invades the human heart. It puts an end to pride and prejudice, it breaks down walls between man and his fellow man, it binds up wounds and cements friendships across all man-made social barriers.

THE EXTERNAL SHAPE DOESN'T MATTER

Jesus said, "Wide is the gate and broad is the road that leads to destruction, and many enter through it."[1] Most people prefer the broad well-paved highway. It beckons the traveller on irresistibly. And who is going to notice big ugly STOP signs, with such a real-looking attractive scene of pleasure ahead?

Those in the speeding car pictured here have already ignored many danger signs along the way. The occupants of the car, drinking, smoking grass, recounting dirty stories, have no interest in the side road that would lead them to life. Nor are they aware of the deep chasm that yawns just behind Satan's masterpiece. Thus the devil has deceived untold multitudes across the years.

In Argentina, a North American Mormon contractor supervised the building of a beautiful church in a town in the interior. Driving back to Cordoba on a country road with his wife to take a plane back to the States, he suddenly saw piles of branches on the road ahead. To those of us who have lived and worked in Argentina for years, it is well known that such branches are the country people's way of warning motorists of danger ahead.

The builder from the North did not know this; so he swerved around the brush pile without slowing down — and plunged into a twelve-foot-deep channel that had been cut through the road by a flash flood. Both were killed and the car destroyed.

Piles of brush in remote regions have often warned us of danger on the road ahead; but in heavily populated areas, highways in Argentina are marked with modern signs.

God has given us big spiritual signs warning us to turn back from our wicked ways. He has given us a conscience that often shouts at us with devastating effect. He uses difficult circumstances to shake us up as we hurtle on to ruin. He sends kind friends who try to get through to us with loving advice. Then there is the word of God, so available, but so often neglected. No wonder the Bible says, "So then, they are without excuse."[2]

[1]Matthew 7:23   [2]Romans 1:20

THE DIABOLICAL PAINTER

The cross of Christ a SWORD? A weapon of aggression? The Old Crusaders thought so. They killed people they called "infidels" with cross-hilted blades.

But they were wrong, weren't they? They failed to heed the words of Christ when he stood trial before Pontius Pilate, "My kingdom is not of this world. If it were, my followers would fight."[1] They ignored the living testimony of the disciples of Jesus, who like Him, allowed themselves to be killed, but refused to kill others.

But the cross is a powerful *spiritual* weapon that dealt the devil a mortal blow. On Mount Calvary, Christ our Lord took upon Himself fallen humanity's sin. He died there that we might live! "For God so loved the world that He gave His one and only Son, that whoever believes in him should not perish but have eternal life."[2] At that moment, God, who is LOVE PERSONIFIED, met Satan who is hate incarnate — and defeated him once and forever.

The cross is a sword that cuts the Gordian knot of sin and sets us free. But it was followed by the resurrection of Christ from the dead! He did die — but He LIVES FOREVERMORE, and is mighty to save all those who call upon Him!

Satan has had his death blow; yet, like most mortally wounded serpents, he is still dangerous. He can still poison the careless and the unbelieving; but, praise the Lord, he cannot harm the one who is wholly given to God, and lives continuously in the shadow of the cross. When Jesus comes back again at the end of this age, all that He accomplished by His death will be completed forever. Then the saying that is written will come true, "Death has been swallowed up in victory."[3]

[1]John 18:36   [2]John 3:16   [3]1 Corinthians 15:54

THE CONQUERING SWORD

151

It's *real!*"

So, after countless empty mirages, a man finds Christ.

My heart aches when I recall some of my closest friends who have drifted blindly past this "living water" and staggered on after mirages — only to die in the burning sands of disappointment, without hope "and without God in the world."[1]

I personally have never wandered far into that desert of illusion. I have not tried the deceptive comforts and thrills of drugs, alcohol or sexual adventures. Admittedly, there used to be times, especially when I was growing up, that the hot colors of worldly living looked very attractive; but only a short way into the desert my thirst for the water of life drew me back to Him; for since the age of five I knew Him.

Long ago our Lord Jesus Christ stood up before Jerusalem's holiday crowd and cried out, "If any man thirsts, let him come to Me and drink."[2] He Himself is still, today, that life-giving *oasis* in the world's desert.

In the barren wilderness of Palestine, David cried out, "My God . . . my soul thirsts for Thee; my flesh yearns for Thee in a dry and weary land where there is no water!"[3] He was like so many who have seen life's promised satisfactions vanish, when almost within reach. But God was there all the time; and David found Him. So did Abraham, centuries before; for Jesus said to King David's descendants, "Your father Abraham rejoiced to see My day, and he saw it and was glad."[4]

[1]Ephesians 2:12   [2]John 7:37   [3]Psalm 63:1   [4]John 8:56

OASIS IN THE DESERT

There may be very little aesthetic beauty or dramatic action in this dual diagram; but it has a vital message for all.

In the picture at the top, rays of lightning are striking all three crosses, the two smaller ones on the outside because they represent condemned criminals who deserved the wrath of God. But why are they striking the cross of Christ? He was holy, undefiled, and separate from sinners! The answer is simple: He was bearing our sins in His own body on the tree; and God was pouring out His punishment for *our* sins on Him there.

Then comes the logical question: "How is it that one of the thieves was saved and went to heaven, while the other was lost and went to hell?" Good question. They were both bad men, condemned by the law. What then made the difference?

When we study the record closely, we see several basic differences. The Word says that at the first, both of these men joined with the Satan-inspired rabble in jeering at Christ. But one changed his tune — why? I believe it was because beneath all the blood and sweat that covered the skeletal body of the tortured Savior, he saw who Christ really was. Who but Jesus would cry out, "Father, forgive them, they know not what they do!"

So later on, during that dread hour, he changed his attitude; and when the other thief, sneering at Jesus, said, "If you are the Christ, save yourself and us," the believing thief rebuked him, saying (in our vernacular), "Look, Bud, keep your big mouth shut. We are here getting what we deserve; but this Man has done nothing wrong." In a word, he confessed his personal guilt. The first step in salvation.

Then he took the second all-important step. He turned to Jesus and cried, "Lord, remember me when you come in your kingdom!" He called upon Jesus. His faith saw, not a tortured victim, but a future King! And what did Jesus reply? *"Today, shall you be with me in paradise."* He didn't say, "I'm sorry, I only save good people." He didn't say, "I'm sorry, but there's a housing shortage in heaven; and next month we're going to call the angels together to vote on it . . ." *"Today . . . with me!"*

UNDER THE SHELTER OF HIS CROSS

155

A great craggy rock can mean disaster to a storm-driven vessel. At the tender age of seven, I saw the rusting hull and leaning mast of a wrecked ocean-going tanker on the Atlantic coast. It made an indelible impression on my little mind. But the same rock that destroys a proud globe-encircling ship can provide protection for a fragile little bird sitting on its nest.

The rugged heights and caves of Judea meant escape and safety for David centuries ago, when he was forced to flee from the army of implacable King Saul. Hunted like a wild animal by the jealous monarch, young David cried out to God, "Be *thou* to me a Rock of strength, a stronghold to save me!"[1]

The Bible is full of references to God as our "Rock." Moses called God "the Rock" whom "Jacob found in a desert land."[2] The Apostle Paul wrote, ". . . That Rock was Christ."[3]

I know how David felt when he cried out, "My soul thirsts for Thee . . . in a dry and weary land where there is no water."[4] One day, after long hours of plodding along on horseback under a blazing desert sun, I rode into a shady canyon of the Sacramento Mountains of New Mexico. Leaving my tired cow pony to drink great draughts from a stagnant pool, I picked my way over the rough terrain to a large cave in the rocky cliff above. There, clear cold water — God's gracious provision — dripped into a sparkling naturally-formed basin. I drank deeply, and gave thanks to my Heavenly Father for that great rock and its cave.

Storm driven by human and satanic forces, the Christian must often flee, like David, to his Spiritual Rock. "I will say of the Lord, He is my refuge and my Fortress, my God, in Him will I trust."[5] In this storm-lashed scene, we can see ourselves as a little bird in his snug dry shelter; and we can say with our little feathered friend, "Let 'er blow!"

[1]Psalm 31:3   [2]Deuteronomy 32:4, 9, 10   [3]1 Corinthians 10:4   [4]Psalm 89:26
[5]Psalm 63:1

"LET 'ER BLOW!"

157

When I was a young lad just beginning to serve the Lord, there was a cartoonist who drew Bible-teaching-type pictures. One of them which I remember vividly to this day pictured the cross as a bridge across a deep chasm. The paper was the *Sunday School Times*, the artist, E.J. Pace.

Some years later I felt led of God to paint this same scene in oils, showing the Holy City of God on the far bank and this world system in flames at the near end.

Perhaps I should not have been surprised, but I was, when many Christians who attended my meetings bought the first rather simple scene in print form. It spoke silently but eloquently to their hearts of the tremendous significance of the cross of Christ. It was a sermon without words.

A pastor in Lansing, Michigan, was in the process of building a new tabernacle-type church at the time that I was invited to hold an evangelistic campaign there. During the week I painted this scene of the cross as a bridge on the large wall behind the pulpit. Some years later, the Sunday School superintendent of that same church told me that he had been converted through that painting. He said that he didn't remember a word of the sermon that night; but couldn't get that picture out of his mind. The Holy Spirit kept it right there!

So, by faith, he stepped out on that great bridge with the others who were moving across it, and was saved! It is a source of deep spiritual satisfaction to me to know that well over 50,000 of these prints have been silently witnessing to many hearts over the years.

But what exactly *is* the message of this allegorical scene? Just this: That Christ, through His death on the cross, constructed an invisible, but very real bridge from the kingdom of darkness to the kingdom of light. This is not just from this present life to the life beyond called heaven; these kingdoms exist today, side by side. By faith we can cross over right now, without waiting until we die.

Jesus Christ said of Himself, "I am the way, the truth and the life; no man comes to the Father but by me."[1] Of course I realize that some will say, "How come Jesus is the *only* way?" The answer is that He was the only true human being who was also God; and being God manifest in the flesh, He, the sinless Son of the Father, could offer Himself as a perfect sacrifice for our sins. Obviously, a sinful person like us cannot pay the debt of sin, since he himself is

[1]John 14:6

THE WAY OF THE CROSS

spiritually bankrupt. Not only so, but one human being, even if he were sinless, could not offer an infinite sacrifice for all humanity. Christ could. And He did!

* * * * *

What a magnificent bridge it is! And best of all — it's for real! Sinful people from the beginning of the human race until now have been saved by the precious blood that was shed on that cross by the Lamb of God, "who takes away the sin of the world."[1]

In Old Testament times, God-seeking men offered lambs without blemish or spot on simple altars. Why? As a visible demonstration of their faith in the One, Jesus, who would come later on in history to be the fulfillment of all of those prototype sacrifices. A helpless little lamb dying on an altar is a very graphic illustration of the innocent suffering for the guilty.

Today it is no longer necessary to offer sacrificial animals, because Christ on the cross, as the Scriptures clearly say, "Offered *one* sacrifice for sins forever, and sat down at the right hand of the Father."[2] Why did He sit down? Elementary. The work of eternal redemption was finished! The Savior on the cross did not cry, "It is *begun!*" He cried, "It is *finished.*"[3]

All of which means that no other sacrifice for sins is necessary, or can be added to His perfect sacrifice. To be saved, we must abandon any and all so-called "good works" of our own, and put all our trust in His complete, perfect and eternal work accomplished gloriously on the hill called Calvary. For it is "not by works of righteousness that we have done; but according to His mercy *He* saved us."[4]

I think you can see by now that this is no doubt the most important cartoon in this book. Believe its message. Accept this, God's gracious offer. He loves you. The cross is the eternal proof of His concern for your eternal welfare.

Let me say, with all humility, that this is not simply a set of doctrines that I have memorized — it is a very real and wonderful experience that has stayed with me for over half a century. If it were just a theoretical religious code, or a shallow emotional "high," I would have come down a long time ago. Praise the Lord, it is for real — and it is for YOU!

[1]Hebrews 10:12   [2]Hebrews 9:14   [3]John 19:30   [4]Titus 3:5

THE MANGER: WHERE ALL ARE WELCOME

DREAMING ABOUT A MAGIC CARPET

THE HIDDEN CHRIST

163

**THE ONLY SOLUTION: RENOUNCE HOMOSEXUAL
PERVERSION**

HOW TO REALLY KICK THE DRUG HABIT

THE EXHAUSTED HORSE

THE INTERNATIONAL PIZZA PARTY

UNUSUAL PROTEST MARCH

BROTHERS UNDER THE SHELL

THE CARELESS AVIATOR

DETHRONING THE ENEMY

THE GREAT CONFRONTATION

172

TALK — OR ACTION?

173

THE TROJAN HORSE

THE RELIGIOUS SUPERSTAR

Prison chaplains are pleading for thousands of Phil Saint's illustrated books, both in Spanish and English. Those who would like to help, send your love offering checks marked "Prison Book Ministry" made out to: Saint Ministries International, Inc. and mail to 2535 New Garden Rd., Greensboro, N.C. 27408.

If you would like to obtain more information concerning the prison ministry, please contact: John A. Fesmire, 451 Waters Rd., Ft. Pierce, FL 34946.

All donations receipted for Income Tax deductions.